P9-CQM-256

STAN TOLER'S PRACTICAL GUIDE TO HIRING STAFF

HOW TO RECRUIT AND RETAIN AN EFFECTIVE MINISTRY TEAM

STAN TOLER

Compliments of...

wesleyan publishing house
P.O. Box 50434
Indianapolis, IN 46250-0434

Call: 800.493.7539 • Fax: 800.788.3535
E-mail: wph@wesleyan.org • Online: www.wesleyan.org/wph
Please send copies of any review or mention.

wesleyan
publishing
house

Indianapolis, Indiana

Copyright © 2009 by Wesleyan Publishing House
Published by Wesleyan Publishing House
Indianapolis, Indiana 46250
Printed in the United States of America
ISBN 978-0-89827-384-7

Library of Congress Cataloging-in-Publication Data

Toler, Stan.
  Stan Toler's practical guide to hiring staff : how to recruit and
retain an effective ministry team / Stan Toler.
    p. cm.
  Includes bibliographical references.
  ISBN 978-0-89827-384-7
  1. Church personnel management. I. Title. II. Title: Practical guide
to hiring staff.
  BV652.13.T66 2009
  254--dc22
                                                    2009013365

To Dr. Thomas H. Hermiz who hired me as his first
staff member when I was a junior in college. A wonderful
mentor, powerful preacher, and superb leader.

CONTENTS

PREFACE

This book is the third in a series of practical guides for pastors, and I am particularly excited about the potential of this book to assist you in your growing ministry.

Many pastors eagerly anticipate the time when their church is ready to transition from a solo pastorate into a multiple staff ministry, but when the day finally arrives, they're not quite sure how to make it all happen. That's where I hope this book will be a great help.

Hiring and managing new staff members require additional knowledge and a different set of skills than are required for solo ministry. First, there is the need to lead the church to the place where they are ready to support and fund the addition of staff. Then, you need to know how to recruit, interview, and select the person that is the best fit for your church and the position. Once a staff member is on board, there is a new layer of responsibility, including mentoring, managing, and holding the staff person accountable. These are not skills pastors or anyone else are given at birth—you have to learn them. The good news is that you *can* learn them; and by learning from those with experience, you can avoid some of the pitfalls and get a head start on a great multi-staff ministry.

When it comes to ministry, I like to say that "It's not about theory, it's about practice." So in addition to key principles and big ideas, my goal is to give you lots of nuts-and-bolts tools that you can use to put the key hiring principles into practice right away.

Transitioning from solo pastor to senior pastor is both an exhilarating and hazardous pathway. I'm grateful to have the privilege of being your companion on the journey. Together we can do it!

STAN TOLER

ACKNOWLEDGMENTS

Many thanks to the team at Wesleyan Publishing House, especially Don Cady, Kevin Scott, Joe Jackson, Rachael Stevenson, and Lyn Rayn. Thanks also to Ron McClung for editorial assistance, and to Deloris Leonard and Pat Diamond. Thank you for helping me elevate this project to a new level.

1

VISION
Making the Case for Multiple Staff

*Moving from a solo pastorate into a multiple staff
ministry requires a compelling vision.*

F our months into office, President John F. Kennedy stood
before Congress and proposed an unprecedented goal for our
country: "I believe this nation should commit itself to the goal,
before this decade is out, of landing a man on the Moon and
returning him safely to Earth."[1]

Almost unthinkable in 1961,
the challenge jarred the scientific
community. As Andrew Chaikin
points out, "Human beings had
barely taken their first toddling
steps off the planet. NASA had just lofted Alan Shepard on a
fifteen-minute suborbital flight. Now Kennedy was giving them
less than nine years to get to the moon."[2]

What motivated the president to issue such an urgent
deadline for reaching the moon? In April 1961, the Soviet

> No man that does not see
> visions will ever realize any
> high hope or undertake
> any high enterprise.
>
> —Woodrow Wilson

Union had sent the first man into space, embarrassing the United States government who believed they possessed superior technology. Space provided a new battleground for the cold war. Kennedy's advisers had told him only a race to land a man on the moon offered the United States a chance to show its superiority over the Russians. Within days after Shepard's flight, Kennedy made his decision and committed our country to winning the space race.

Sixteen months later, he spoke at Rice University stadium on the outskirts of Houston, Texas, to help dedicate the National Aeronautics and Space Administration's new Manned Spacecraft Center some twenty-two miles away. Anticipating the many questions that would arise, Kennedy proposed his own queries: "Why choose this as our goal? And they may well ask, Why climb the highest mountain? Why, thirty-five years ago, fly the Atlantic?"[3]

Think of it: Less than thirty-five years after Charles Lindbergh flew his tiny plane across the Atlantic, serious thinkers discussed flying to the moon. And only forty-two years after Lindbergh's flight, it was done! Neil Armstrong set foot on the moon on July 20, 1969.

Kennedy further told his audience at Rice University that the first voyages in space would be "in some measure an act of faith and vision, for we do not know what benefits await us." He continued: "We choose to go to the moon! We choose to go to the moon in this decade and do the other things—*not* because they are easy, but because they are *hard*. Because that goal will serve to organize and measure the best of our abilities and skills, because that challenge is one that we are willing to accept, one we are unwilling to postpone, and one which we intend to win."[4]

Kennedy's speeches and the subsequent successful mission to the moon provide a classic example of what happens when people commit themselves to accomplish the impossible, and then marshal all available forces to do it.

To move from a solo pastorate into a multi-staff operation in a local church may seem as challenging to you as putting a man on the moon. Considering the financial costs involved, the change required in getting board and congregations to think differently about how the church does ministry, and other potential pitfalls, it's enough to put a pastor into orbit!

Discerning the Need for Multiple Staff

A friend told me about a pastor who declared, "I have about a hundred people in my church and a hundred is enough. That's about how many I can handle. I really don't want any more."

To say the least, such a pastor has little vision. But let's face it: When a church exceeds a hundred people in attendance, a solo pastor begins to feel the pressure of trying to minister to all the people all the time. A few people in the hospital at the same time, especially if parishioners use multiple hospitals in more than one city, can leave pastors frazzled, trying to be sure they cover all the bases.

Don't Settle for Average

Why is the average church in America approximately one hundred in attendance? Some observers think it's because that's

⊹⊱━ ━⊰⊹
Vision and Visionaries

Leaders do not have to be the greatest visionaries themselves. The vision may come from anyone. The leaders do have to state the vision, however. Leaders also have to keep the vision before the people and remind them of the progress that is being made to achieve the vision. Otherwise, the people might assume that they are failing and give up.

—Ezra Earl Jones

about how many parishioners one pastor can minister to without adding staff. To grow beyond one hundred members forces a pastor to develop a more complex organizational structure. Improving organization, finding enough volunteer leaders, or supervising staff involves much more work. It's easier to be satisfied as a solo pastor with an average church.

For a local church to move beyond this level of comfort, the pastor will have to cast a vision for it. Unless the pastor casts a vision for multiple staff, most churches will assume the pastor should still "do it all."

Answer Four Questions

Veteran church consultant Carl George suggests four questions to ask in developing and presenting a vision to a church. The first is "What?" What do you see that God wants you to accomplish in your place of ministry? If you don't sense a vision from God for a ministry that's too big for one pastor, don't even think about presenting the idea of multiple staff to your board.

The second question is "How?" How does God want it done? In various Old Testament accounts, God not only told his people what he wanted them to do, but often told them how to do it.

The third question is "Whom?" By whom should the vision be accomplished? God even determined at times who should be involved in the process of getting the job done. He declared, "Judah shall go first" in fighting against the Benjamites (Judg. 20:13–18).

The fourth question is "When?" God sometimes moves very quickly and other times asks his servants to wait. God's timing is important, especially when adding the first staff member. I've seen churches move too quickly, or not screen their candidates thoroughly enough, or rush to find any warm body. When the first staff person you add doesn't perform well or proves not to be a good fit, it may be a long time before the church will be ready to try it again. If you bring it up, you'll hear, "We tried that before and it didn't work."

In addition, some pastors try to expand staff before the church has its finances in order or before they've enlisted sufficient support for the idea. Sometimes a church board will allow the pastor to do what he wants, and only later does the pastor discover they were not supportive of the idea.[5]

+⇒= =⇐+

Pitfalls to Avoid in the Visioning Process

First, without a vision there is no target. It is impossible to move toward a target if one is not defined.

Second, multiple visions create confusion. "The 'default strategy' for many businesses (or churches) seems to be 'advance until fired upon.' In other words, there is no strategy except to keep moving in the current direction and hope."*

Finally, there is the need for the right vision. A wrong vision leads to frustration and stagnation.

—Adapted from *Mobilizer*, vol. 7, no. 2

*Karl Albrecht, *The Northbound Train* (New York: American Management Association, 1994), 2.

Vision Casters in the Bible

The Bible is full of people who had visions and then communicated them. In fact, the Lord said through Jeremiah, "Let the prophet who has a dream tell his dream" (Jer. 23:38). Actually, if a prophet has a dream, it's difficult to stop him from telling the dream. As the Lord said in the next verse, "Is not my word like fire . . . and like a hammer that breaks a rock in pieces?" (Jer. 23:39). A poised hammer is prepared to strike and a burning fire is hard to quench.

Be advised, however, that in communicating a vision for change in the church's long-standing structure, it's better to let the fire illuminate than to let it burn. It's better if one's hammer is velvet covered, not for bashing heads, but for driving home the point.

Joseph, the Dreamer

Joseph is well known as a dreamer. As a young man, his vision irritated his older brothers. Joseph dreamed that he and his ten brothers were binding sheaves of grain in the field. Suddenly his sheaf rose up and the others bowed down to it. At best, Joseph was naïve to think his brothers would not resent his dream and its interpretation. At worst, he took delight in letting them know he believed he would supersede them. Whatever his motive, his brothers "hated him all the more because of his dream and what he had said" (Gen. 37:8). It's a reminder that we need to communicate our dreams with humility, not with pride or any sense of entitlement.

Over the years, Joseph experienced many trials. His troubles tempered and matured him. When the time came to interpret the Egyptian pharaoh's dream, his interpretation revealed he had become a man of wisdom; he found favor with the king (Gen. 41:39 40).

The ancient wise man observed that a vision for God's plan is crucial: "Where there is no vision, the people perish" (Prov. 29:18 KJV). If a pastor has a limited vision of a church where only he serves in a ministerial capacity, he may become the greatest hindrance to that church's growth and development. The church will never grow beyond his vision. In the meantime, he stunts his own growth when his vision is too small. Not every church will become a multiple-staff church. But many more could be, if the pastor's vision expanded to include a team of workers instead of solo ministry.

Paul, the Servant

By contrast, Paul told King Agrippa, "I was not disobedient to the vision from heaven" (Acts 26:19). The vision God gave him on the road to Damascus changed his life. He went on to accomplish great things, usually in partnership with his "staff." Men such as Timothy, Titus, Luke, Silas, and others enhanced his ministry. In fact, he said, "I was glad when Stephanas, Fortunatus and Achaicus arrived. . . . For they refreshed my spirit and yours also. Such men deserve recognition" (1 Cor. 16:17–18). Paul believed in multiple-staff ministry.

Peter, the Preacher

The prophet Joel foresaw the day when the Lord would pour out his Spirit "on all people. Your sons and daughters will prophesy, your old men will dream dreams, your young men will see visions. Even on my servants, both men and women, I will pour out my Spirit in those days" (Joel 2:28–29).

When Peter cited that passage on the Day of Pentecost and applied it to his generation, the results were breathtaking as the three thousand people who "accepted his message were baptized, and . . . added to their number that day" (Acts 2:41). A vision, well communicated, is a powerful thing.

Jesus, the Ultimate Visionary

Jesus, of course, not only had a vision for what God wanted, but he communicated it with great clarity. "When he saw the crowds, he had compassion on them." Why? Because he saw "they were harassed and helpless, like sheep without a shepherd" (Matt. 9:36–37). His own shepherd's heart was so moved that he not only envisioned the work he could do for the sheep, but the work each of us can do—he calls us to be shepherds of his flock.

Elmer Towns observes that Jesus' vision of people motivated him to action. It motivated him to preach his greatest sermon, the Sermon on the Mount. His vision of people also motivated him to give his greatest call for prayer, a prayer for workers (Matt. 9:38). His vision further inspired his greatest challenge, a call to make disciples of all nations (Matt. 28:18–20).[6]

The biblical precedents for receiving and communicating vision should encourage every pastor to seek the Lord's direction and timing for expanding staff.

Communicating the Vision

Once a pastor has determined the vision the church should pursue, he has the responsibility of communicating it, first to the board or the ruling authority of the church and then to the congregation. Fred Smith cautions leaders to be sure their vision comes from the heart. It must not be something they think the church wants them to say. Smith calls such insincere leaders "'clouds without rain.' In a parched land, they look promising. But they float on over, bringing only a shadow."[7]

Several key ideas will help pastors clarify and communicate their vision more effectively.

Discern the Preferred Future

Your overall vision for the church should answer the question, "When we fulfill the Great Commission in this place, what will it look like?" Your vision is a picture of what the ideal ministry looks like in the place where God has called you.

Vision is more than looking into the future. As Rick Warren points out, "Most people think of vision as the ability to see the future. But in today's rapidly changing world, vision is also the ability to creatively assess current changes and take advantage of them. Vision is being alert to opportunities."[8]

What opportunities do you see that you can't take advantage of because you lack sufficient staff? As you consider the

> **The Hope of the World**
>
> A vision without a task is but a dream; a task without a vision is drudgery; a vision and a task is the hope of the world.
>
> —from a church in Sussex, England, 1730

opportunities, formulate a vision of what could be if you had another staff person on board. A vision's power rests, at least in part, on its ability to create *buy-in*: "When people buy into your dreams, they buy into your leadership."[9]

While vision is more than looking into the future, it's a way of predicting a *preferred* future. Some historians believe President McKinley was a great statesman because he could put his ear to the ground and listen for things that were coming. "He turned his listening into vision. He saw what lay ahead."[10] Use your envisioning skills to think ahead and determine, as best you can, how your vision will affect the future of your church.

Examine Your Motives

I mentioned earlier that some churches try to move into a multiple-staff situation too soon. Ask yourself: Is this best for the church and its ministry, or am I anxious to become a senior pastor for more personal reasons? There's no magic number as to what size your church should be before you consider multiple staff, but I have often wondered why a church of seventy persons needs more than one pastor. If the church has no qualified laypersons to work with young people or lead worship or direct Christian education, perhaps this justifies a part-time staff person. Except in unusual situations, moving into multiple staff at that level may stretch a church's finances beyond its capabilities. Be sure such a move is in the church's best interest. Don't make that move to stroke your own ego.

Crystallize Your Thoughts

Phil Stevenson says, "If you are unable to articulate the vision in a few sentences you do not understand it."[11] Better yet, write it down. Writing forces you to be specific; it helps you avoid fuzziness in your thinking. If you can't write it, you need to do more research, more analysis, and more creative thinking. Don't be afraid to think great thoughts. British statesman Benjamin Disraeli declared, "Nurture great thoughts, for you will never go higher than your thoughts."[12] Then be sure it's God's idea, not just a recommendation from the latest megachurch spokesperson. What works there may or may not work for you. Your vision needs to be unique to your church.

Portray a Clear Image

A vision is a word picture. What images or metaphors can you use to help others understand what you feel God is saying to you? If you want to expand staff, you need a clear picture of what that person will do.

Five Keys to Casting Vision

1. Do it pictorially. A vision is visual in nature. What kind of picture does your vision create in people's minds?
2. Do it passionately. If you are not excited about where you're going, don't expect anyone to follow.
3. Do it precisely. The vision must be clear and focused. Spell out details or give the people a concrete image of the vision.
4. Do it prominently. The vision has to be given high visibility. Cast it from the pulpit, the bulletin, and the newsletter.
5. Do it painstakingly. Casting a vision takes planning and effort, with continuity and repetition. The vision must be perceived as more than a flash-in-the-pan pipe dream.

—Jim Dethmer

21

Ken Blanchard has observed, "World-class athletes often visualize themselves breaking a world record, pitching a perfect game, or making a 99-yard punt return. They know that power comes from having a clear mental picture of their best performance potential."[13]

Further, ask yourself, "If I fulfill my vision and hire another staff member, how will it help the church?" What contribution will this person make to the kingdom? How will the church be better off if we hire another person? Your board and congregation will be asking these questions.

Cast and Recast

Bill Hybels, founding pastor of Willow Creek Community Church, admitted, "I have consistently underestimated how often I need to rekindle and to redramatize the vision."[14]

Rick Warren has developed several ways to present the purposes of the church. He believes the vision of any church "always fades with time unless it is reinforced. This is because people become distracted by other things. Restate your purposes on a regular basis."[15] Warren uses Scripture, symbols, slogans, and stories to keep his vision fresh before the people.

When you tire of repeating the vision, remember what Max DePree said: "You have to act like a third-grade teacher. You have to repeat the vision over and over again until people get it right!"[16]

Making the Vision a Reality

Once you've formulated your vision for expanding staff, determined how to express it, and understand the need for repeating it, what steps will make that vision a reality?

Seek Early Buy-In

Before you approach the governing board with your dream, recruit people of influence as allies in your cause. When you persuade people of influence, they can help you sell the project to the board. If your most influential leaders are opposed to the idea, it's too soon to present it to the board. I cannot exaggerate the importance of having "the meeting before the meeting."

Over lunch or coffee, share your heart with leaders of influence. They may suggest ideas that reinforce the dream or they may offer objections you will need to overcome. By spotting the flaws in your plan, they will be doing you a favor. Do some more homework, correct the flaws, or gather information to address the weaknesses before going public with your ideas.

Fred Smith advises a leader to "coagulate followers around the vision, not around himself."[17] His distinction

Undergrowth that Chokes Vision

Vision can become a liability if not tended carefully; be alert to toxic weeds.

The Dream Weed
Healthy daydreams can turn destructive if they cause us to desire the impossible. Such dreams grow out of our frustration, anger, and self pity. A dose of reality is an effective antidote.

The Greed Weed
Desiring one's church to prosper is a good thing—until the vision includes a new car and a bigger salary. Greed is impatient; the best weapon against it is patience.

The Hero Weed
Too often, our own faces figure prominently in our dreams. We see ourselves heroically restoring a dying church. To extract our ego from our vision, engage in private prayer.

—adapted from an article by David Hansen

makes a good point, because you want people who are allied to your vision, not tied to your personality. Then, when they agree with your vision, they're not doing you a favor; they're doing what is right for the kingdom.

Paint a Picture

When influential leaders have expressed agreement, it's time to share your vision with the governing board. In persuading the board that staff expansion will improve the church's ministry, be careful how you frame your ideas.

Don't emphasize how a new staff member will help you personally. Don't talk about how much time and energy it's going to save you, although that is part of the mix.

Don't talk about how it will make your job easier. For one thing, there's nothing easy about supervising staff. Although your workload may change—more supervision, less direct involvement in certain ministries—it won't be easier.

Anyway, it's not about you as the senior pastor, even if you do feel overworked and underpaid. It's about being more effective in meeting the needs of the congregation and the community.

To be sure, many pastors work too hard and put in too many hours. But unless you've just had a heart attack or some other serious physical problem, most people will not see your health as the issue.

Show the benefits to the church. Adding staff will cost more money and affect the way the church has always done things. Therefore you must show the board how this change will benefit the church. Talk about how it will improve the church's effectiveness. Talk about what the church will be able to do that it can't do now. Determine what specific needs the new staff person will meet. What problems will it solve? What age groups will benefit? What ministries will a new staff member enhance?

Communicate with enthusiasm and joy. If you can't speak with enthusiasm about your dream, don't expect anyone else to get excited about it. Solomon uttered wisdom when he said, "Whatever your hand finds to do, do it with all your might" (Eccl. 9:10).

Ralph Waldo Emerson wrote, "To the dull mind all nature is leaden. To the illumined mind the whole world burns and sparkles with light." It's your job to illumine the board members until your vision sparkles in their minds.

Communicate clearly and concisely. Theodore Hesburgh said, "The very essence of leadership is [that] you have to have a vision. It's got to be a vision you articulate clearly and forcefully on every occasion. You can't blow an uncertain trumpet."[18]

Steps to Sharing the Vision

1. Define the target. Who needs to hear the vision? This is both the core and those you are wanting to join the core.

2. Share vision development. Never develop your vision in a vacuum. Let others participate in refining and chiseling it. When people have input, their output increases.

3. Overspeak the vision. Repeat the vision regularly and differently. Use all modes of communication.

4. Simple is better. Remember the three "S's": Short, Simple, Snappy.

5. Be the vision. You must model the vision. Nothing communicates vision like seeing it lived out in the life of the leader.

—adapted from Phil Stevenson

Live the Vision Personally

If you're a pastor who gives himself without reservation to the ministry, your people will know you're serious about the work of the kingdom. As you bring people to Christ, baptize them, welcome them into membership, and lead the church in discipling them, the congregation will know you are passionate about the church. More than a vocation, it's a calling.

When they see these things, they'll understand that you want to enlist staff members with a similar calling, passion, and work ethic. They'll know you aren't building your own kingdom, but the kingdom of Christ.

In short, when you live it, they will see it.

Tie the Vision to Eternal Values

Many things we do in the church will not outlive us nor have lasting impact. But hiring church staff has eternal consequences. Staff members sit on a pedestal. They are more visible than the average church member. Their actions have greater impact. When staff members fail or fall, the ripple effect may continue for years.

By stressing this to your leaders, you will help them see you approach the matter with soberness. By emphasizing the eternal element, you stress the importance of finding the right person for this time in the church's history. You're saying, "This person will influence our children [or youth or worship or whatever their area of concentration] for years to come." We want to make these decisions well.

The Greatest Enterprise

Larry King tells about interviewing Tommy Lasorda, manager of the Los Angeles Dodgers, the night after his team lost to Houston in the 1981 National League playoffs. Lasorda was so enthusiastic in the interview that King asked him how he could be so exuberant after losing such a crucial game.

Lasorda answered, "The best day of my life is when I manage a winning game. And the second best day of my life is when I manage a losing game."[19]

Be sure you have accurate facts and figures when you approach your board. Be sure you have thought through both advantages and disadvantages for adding staff. Be sure you have developed allies who will help you sell your vision. Be thoroughly convinced that your vision will greatly benefit the church. Then whatever happens—win or lose—know that you are involved in the greatest enterprise on earth—the Church of the Lord Jesus Christ.

Victor Frankl was a successful Viennese psychiatrist when the Nazis threw him into a concentration camp. After the war, this survivor gave a speech in which he said,

There is only one reason why I am here today. What kept me alive was you. Others gave up hope. I dreamed. I dreamed that someday I would be here, telling you how I, Victor Frankl, had survived the Nazi concentration camps. I've never been here before, I've never seen any of you before, I've never given this speech before. But in my dreams, I have stood before you and said these words a thousand times.[20]

Such is the power of a vision. Dream on.

Action Steps

1. Write out your specific vision for multiple staff in your church.
2. List the objections people may have to expanding staff.
3. What specific answers do you have for those objections? Write them down.
4. Who are the influential leaders you need to talk with about your vision?
5. Set up a meeting with the leaders you need to bring on board.

2

APPROPRIATION
Funding the Staffing Plan

It's one thing to dream of additional staff.
It's quite another to find the extra dollars to pay for it.

Pastor John sat slumped over his desk, head in hands, half-praying and half-lamenting what had proven to be a poor plan. The year before, several families had moved away due to job transfers, corporate downsizing, and subsequent layoffs. Still, the finance committee chose not to make adjustments when setting the budget for the current year, believing they would add new families and offset the loss of tithes. When church offerings dropped below budget, they dipped into the church's considerable savings account to pay staff salaries and "keep the ship afloat." Though the church had reached some new people, they didn't give at the same level, and the budget was still underfunded. Now, the savings were almost gone and morale was at an all-time low.

> Churches often fail to count the hidden costs of poor salaries.
>
> —Wayne Pohl

How could the church have avoided such a predicament? What should the pastor have done? Our advice won't help Pastor John right now, except to serve as guidelines for the future, but let's explore the considerations involved in paying for additional staff.

Economic Challenges of Adding Staff

Did Pastor John and his finance committee step out on faith, or did they move forward with presumption? Anyone who ignores the facts and fails to deal with the realities of the church's economic struggles will live to regret it.

Difference of Opinion

Funding staff expansion is no picnic except in those rare cases when the economy is booming, church attendance is spiraling upward, and money is coming in faster than we can spend it.

Wayne Pohl tells about a time in the early 1980s when his city was hit hard by a recession and layoffs. Several families in the church were unemployed. Ironically the church was doing well financially. Both membership and giving had increased the previous year.

The elder board agonized over what to do about staff pay increases. With such impressive gains, normally they would have been generous. But how would it appear to give the staff significant increases when several in the congregation were unemployed? They finally decided on modest increases, somewhat less than they would have given under normal circumstances.

The next morning, an elder told Wayne he had decided to resign because he could not live with the pay increases. He felt they were excessive, given the hardship many in the congregation were enduring. Wayne asked him to take a week to think and pray before deciding.

That afternoon another elder knocked on his door and informed him he was going to resign because he felt the pay increases were too small. He felt they were penalizing the staff after such an outstanding year. Wayne asked him to take a week to think and pray before deciding.

Both men changed their minds and stayed on the elder board. But this illustrates how difficult it is to arrive at a decision about staff salaries that everyone can support.[1]

Congregational Support

In an interview I was asked this question: "Under what conditions would you discourage a church from conducting a [capital stewardship] campaign?" I answered, "At least two things must be in place before a capital stewardship campaign is launched: One, the church must have a vision for the project under consideration; and two, the congregation should have a strong sense of unity for the project."[2]

I believe the same two conditions should exist before a church expands its staff. If the senior pastor has not cast a vision and convinced his congregation of the need for expanded staff, the church is not likely to have a sense of unity over adding to the payroll. Without unity, or at least an overwhelming consensus, they will never give the added dollars needed to fund more staff.

The Cost of Hiring . . . and Not Hiring

As I mentioned in the previous chapter, churches are sometimes prone to expand staff before they have a clear picture of how they will handle the additional financial load. What will the new staff member's compensation involve? Will it include housing allowance, pension, health insurance, Social Security reimbursement (in the case of clergy), and an allowance for professional expenses, such as mileage reimbursement, book purchases, and subscriptions to professional magazines?

> **Rich Topsoil for Growing Dollars**
>
> The richest topsoil for growing dollars for ministry is a vision for the Great Commission. If I have cast the vision clearly, if our hearts are beating for the lost, finances will follow. Money flows to the right causes.
>
> —Wayne Pohl

In addition to asking how much it will cost to hire a new staff person, the flip side is what will it cost us not to hire? And what will it cost us if we hire, but don't pay the person well? I hear stories about families who leave a church because it doesn't have dynamic programs for children or youth. Or families look for a church that has attractive ministries for their children. Unless a church has unusually gifted laypersons, it typically requires staff expansion to provide such ministries.

Who knows how many staff members have "felt the call of God" to relocate to another church, when in reality they felt the call of a better pay package? When staff members move to larger churches, it gives them broader opportunities to work with more people. But usually the larger church is able to pay better as well.

A board member asked why the church kept losing good staff members to larger churches. The pastor answered, "Let's face it. We have become an excellent farm club, providing experience and training for our staff to launch into larger ministries."

Biblical Guidance on Paying Staff

Jesus said we should count the cost. "Suppose one of you wants to build a tower. Will he not first sit down and estimate the cost to see if he has enough money to complete it? For if he lays the foundation and is not able to finish it, everyone who sees it will ridicule him, saying, 'This fellow began to build and was not able to finish'" (Luke 14:28–30).

If we launch into staff expansion without taking an adequate look at how we're going to finance it, we too could be subject to ridicule.

Hiring Foolishly

The Scripture gives examples of those who hired foolishly. Abimelech, hungry for power, convinced his uncles that he was worthy of leading them. Consequently, they gave him money from their temple treasury— admittedly a pagan temple—and he abused the privilege in order to hire mercenaries to further his cause. The Scripture account tells us, "So they gave him seventy shekels of silver from the temple of

> **The Cost of a Bad Hire**
>
> Research in the field of business suggests that the cost of a bad hire— in lost time, money, and customers—can be three to five times the employee's salary. . . . In the case of churches, the loss is not only financial but may mean ruined lives, lost momentum, and fruitlessness in fulfilling Christ's commission to "seek and save the lost."
>
> —Gary L. McIntosh

Baal-Berith, with which Abimelech hired worthless and reckless men; and they followed him" (Judg. 9:4 NKJV).

Generous Compensation

There is no question that the Bible teaches us to pay those who labor in the Lord's vineyard a fair wage. When Jesus appointed the seventy-two and sent them out two by two, he gave specific instructions as to their conduct. If anyone was generous enough to offer them lodging and food, they were to accept it. "Stay in that house," he told them, "eating and drinking whatever they give you, for the worker deserves his wages" (Luke 10:7).

Although the apostle Paul was a bivocational minister who worked as a tentmaker to support his ministry, he instructed Timothy, "The elders who direct the affairs of the church well are worthy of double honor, especially those whose work is preaching and teaching." Quoting Deuteronomy 5:4, he added, "For the Scripture says, 'Do not muzzle the ox while it is treading out the grain,'" and then quoted Jesus, "The worker deserves his wages" (1 Tim. 5:18).

God's Human Agents

People are God's human agents for ministry effectiveness (1 Cor. 3:5–9). Your ministry will be only as good as the people who serve the Lord and the church. Scripture is clear that the workers deserve their wages. . . . It's unbiblical (and shameful) when a church fails to take care of its staff.

—Aubrey Malphurs and Steve Strope

Some commentators believe the "double honor" refers to respect and remuneration. Others think the phrase is about quantity, and literally means the elders "who direct the affairs of the church," especially those who preach and teach, should receive twice as much as other elders. The Jewish birthright customs dictated that the elder son received a double portion of the inheritance.[3] In any case, the Scriptures call for fair, even generous, compensation for those who make their living by working for the Church.

Some have pointed out that Paul's allusions are not very flattering to church leaders. In the one case, he compares pastors to threshing oxen, and in the other he compares them to farm laborers. Paul intends no insult. He is simply saying that pastoral work is difficult and the pastor deserves to be compensated. As John Stott points out, "If God is concerned that working animals are adequately fed, how much more concern must he have for church workers?"[4] And, we might add, how much more concern should we have for those who work hard for the Lord?

The Value of a Staff Person

When we begin to think about funding the vision for expanded staff, the first question that comes to many minds is, "What can we afford?" The better question might be, "What's a great staff person worth?"

Consultant and writer Dale Dauten tells about Kip Tindell, president of The Container Store chain, a company that pays their store personnel double the industry average. Tindell declares one of the company's foundation principles: "One great person equals three good people."[5] Most churches are not capable of paying double the average across the country, but all of us can be on the lookout for great people who will add greater value to our churches than what we can afford to pay them.

Pohl believes the right person will pay for himself or herself within two years.[6] He admits this is based on his strategy of looking for achievers. Staff members who achieve tend to pay for themselves, and then some. So in addition to considering an individual's position, experience, and education, all of which are important, a senior pastor cannot afford to overlook the potential staff member's record of achievement.

Conversely, hiring the wrong person can be costly. For instance, a secretary with poor phone skills can hurt the image of the church. Custodians who constantly complain about the wear and tear on the facilities, and especially if they reprimand the church members, will cost more than they are worth.[7]

Jack Connell tells about a bad hire he made. Before hiring the new staff member, Jack talked with a friend who was the senior pastor at a similar-sized church. Jack asked him about the salary for a comparable position in his church. When his friend gave a number, Jack knew he was not about to offer a salary anywhere near that nigh. He intended to fill the position and save money at the same time.

Adequate Compensation

Most of our staff are younger men with young families; this means mouths to feed, bodies to clothe, and brains to educate. If someone leaves, we want it to be because he has a valid call from God, not because of inadequate compensation.

—Lane Adams

He hired Derik (not the staff person's real name) for about $20,000 less in annual compensation than the number Jack's friend had suggested. When he let Derik go six months later, he had to admit that "being cheap with compensation cost us a lot more than we saved."

Jack acknowledges the hard costs of Derik's severance package, along with additional moving and search expenses. He also acknowledges the soft costs: loss of ministry momentum, stress and strain in his own life, staff disruption. "I can't begin to put a price tag on all of that," Jack confesses, "but the number would clearly be north of $20,000."[8]

Financial Stewardship Myths

How much we pay our staff members and how we raise the funds are issues directly related to our philosophy of stewardship. Consider these myths, proposed by Herb Miller:[9]

1. Christians automatically commit themselves to generous financial stewardship. Not true! There is very little about the Christian life that is automatic. People develop sound giving habits through education, repeated decisions, and their own personal growth.

2. If worship attendance is high, the money takes care of itself. Wish it were so! If people are in the habit of dropping a ten or twenty in the offering plate, ignoring the Scriptures' admonitions to tithe, the church will not prosper.

3. Our people are giving all they can. Hardly! What church is giving 100 percent of its tithe potential? In other words, if you could add all the salaries of all the people who attend the church and divide by ten, that would be the tithe potential. Very few churches are achieving this. In fact, a Barna report in one recent year showed only 5 percent of Americans tithed their pretax income to a church. When asking only those who claimed to be born again, the figure rose to 7 percent.[10]

+≻== =≺+

A Generous Example

Generous givers are led
by generous pastors.
You can't lead people
to generosity except by
example.

—Patrick Johnson

4. Telling people "Our church needs the money!" produces generous giving. Usually not! A better approach appeals to the motivation for giving out of gratitude for God's blessings, love for God, obedience to Scripture, or to help hurting people. Church loyalty and a desire to balance the budget are not typically good motivators for generous giving.

5. People will increase their giving to support our increased budget needs without our annually asking them to consider doing so. Not historically so! In churches that do not conduct annual stewardship campaigns, giving tends to stay the same, even if the parishioners' income increases. An annual campaign typically results in increases in giving. It's the annual "ask" that makes the difference.

6. Our church should use methods that work well in civic organizations and philanthropic causes. Not true! According to Miller, fund raising for nonprofit organizations in the community is "as different from Christian stewardship as a bicycle is from an eighteen-wheeler. Both are valid forms of transportation, but they are not interchangeable."[11] Churches that have high per capita giving are those that use spiritual methods, not fund-raising methods, to challenge people to give.

7. Our members will give generously without our teaching the biblical principle that giving money is an essential part of spiritual growth. Wishful thinking! A solid biblical theology of giving along with a consistent annual stewardship program combine to be the most effective way to motivate Christians to give.

So a church's ability to pay its staff well depends on its ability to continue motivating its members to be faithful, biblical, and sacrificial givers.

Practical Steps to Increase Funding

What are some steps toward motivating a church to become a congregation of generous givers and increase its commitment to support staff?

Track Giving Patterns

What has been the church's giving pattern over the past five years? This will help you determine about what you can expect over the next year or two. If the church plateaus, it's not likely they will give additional funds to support a new staff person, unless you can introduce some unusual level of motivation. On the other hand, if giving has averaged increasing 10 percent per year over the past five years, you might well expect the giving to increase 10 percent next year. Is that enough to afford an additional staff member? If not, do you have enough flexibility in your budget, along with the anticipated increase, to add more staff?

Next look at the church's per capita giving. Is it increasing? Even if attendance has not increased, has the per capita giving

Giving as an Act of Worship

Many people don't understand the basics of financial management, such as establishing and living within a budget or balancing a checkbook, much less the biblical perspective on what to do with one's money. Many church members have been indoctrinated into a payment-for-services-rendered mindset rather than understanding tithing as an act of worship.

—Bruce Anderson

increased? For instance, if you have experienced growth from $1,600 to $1,700 per person last year, and another increase to $1,800 this year, and if you still have high morale and good momentum, you might expect another growth of $100 per person next year.

Look at your attendance. Increasing or decreasing? If it has increased 5 percent per year over the past five years, how many new people will another 5 percent mean for next year? Multiply that by your per capita giving, allowing for the fact that new people don't always give as generously as established people, and arrive at a reasonable estimate as to how much more money you will have to work with over the next twelve months. Is it enough to afford another person on staff?

For those who think this is too mechanical and does not allow for faith, remember that you're projecting faith when you anticipate the growth you expect to come next year. None of us have any guarantees, but if your people have been faithful and God is showing you favor, it's legitimate to make a faith projection.

Budget for Generous Compensation

The responsibility for raising funds in a church belongs squarely with the senior pastor. You may have an excellent finance committee or board of elders to work with you, but you have the opportunity and responsibility to cast a vision for a budget that is generous with staff compensation. If possible, provide increases for current staff. If you're the only current staff, the suggestion for increase will come better from someone else. However, I have known senior pastors who requested a cost-of-living increase when no one seemed to be forthcoming about a raise.

Conduct an Annual Stewardship Campaign

Churches that use an annual stewardship campaign—in which the pastor preaches about tithing as the biblical standard for giving and then asks people to register what they will give—will see a 10 to 15 percent increase in total giving each year. One of the keys is to show the biblical foundation for tithing. Another is to ask, via a commitment card. Obviously, names and commitment amounts are not published. But getting people to sign on the dotted line is crucial. Making the presentation without asking for a commitment usually results in a much lower dollar response.

Teach Biblical Stewardship

A Learned Habit

Generosity is a learned habit, which is why churches must regularly teach about stewardship.

—D. Michael Lindsay

Rick Warren says, "We easily miss the spiritual significance of giving money. We need to give the first part of our day in meditation to God. We need to give the first part of our week in worship of God. We need to give the first part of our income to God. We need to give the first part of our social life to fellowship with other Christians."[12]

Studies have shown that when churches ask, "What percentage of your income is God calling you to give?", their people contribute a higher percentage of their income than those churches that do not ask such questions.

Reward Good Performance

When staff members perform well and the ministries over which they preside flourish, they should be rewarded. If, regardless of performance, everyone receives the same increase, this is a distortion of biblical teaching. The person who performs well may be discouraged. After all, why work harder when someone who is coasting receives the same raise in pay? Of course, we should all be working for the Lord's approval, regardless of what others do and regardless of compensation. But people are human, and such discrepancies may provide an opening for the enemy to sow dissension.

Build Faithful Disciples

The problem with any type of motivation is that it tends to get old. We push attendance and when we stop, it falls back down. We push giving and if we turn our attention to other things, it tends to fall back down. The challenge is always to keep all the plates spinning at the same time.

The better approach is to work on building better people. Waldo Werning said, "Raise men—lift them up! Inspire their spirits! And they'll support your ever-increasing cash needs!"[13]

The Hard Decisions

Across town from Pastor John, Pastor Gary's church had faced similar problems with families facing layoffs and moving away. However, he and his finance committee had seen it coming and, painful though it was, gave one staff member the option of cutting back to part-time or trying to find another full-time job elsewhere. The staff person chose to leave and Pastor Gary hired a part-time person to fill the position. The resultant savings enabled them to survive a difficult year with budgetary integrity. Morale took a small dip after the full-time staff person left, but the part-timer worked hard to keep the ministry viable and morale increased.

Like the man in the story Jesus told, count the cost of adding staff. If your church is growing, you can make a valid case for adding staff; then begin to work with your board to figure out how you can fund it.

It's somewhat like walking a tightrope. If you plunge into staff ministry too soon, you fall off one side. If you wait too long, you miss opportunities, falling off on the other side. Consistent prayer, asking for God's guidance, and carefully seeking godly counsel from your team of advisers will help you walk the tightrope, fund the expansion, and see the church move forward.

Action Steps

1. Track your church's giving and attendance over the past five years. Be sure to include a study of per capita giving trends.

2. Plan for your next annual stewardship campaign. When will you have it? What will your theme be?

3. What lay leaders do you need to consult about budgeting for your next staff person? When will you meet with them?

4. Plan to teach your board and/or finance committee the truths contained in the "financial stewardship myths" in this chapter.

3

TIMING
Knowing When to Hire Staff

Timing is everything.

In Great Britain, elections must be held at least every five years, but sometimes they occur more frequently. The reason is that the British system allows for the administration currently in power to determine the timing of the next election, so long as they do not allow themselves more than five years in power before holding the next election. The temptation for those in power is to try to time the election so that they are most likely to win.

> You know, sometimes, when they say you're ahead of your time, it's just a polite way of saying you have a real bad sense of timing.
>
> —George McGovern

In actual practice, that's not as simple as it sounds. More than once, the administration in office has thought it would be a good time to hold an election and that they would easily retain power, only to be surprised by the results. For instance in May 1970, the British Labour Party rose in the public opinion polls ahead of the Conservative Party for the first time in three years. Labour Prime Minister Harold McMillan, intending to take advantage of Labor's sudden popularity, called a quick election. He was surprised when Conservatives surged at the ballot box and won 330 of 630 seats.[1]

Similar surprises happen in the United States, even though elections are held consistently every four years. In the early 1990s, President George H. W. Bush's popularity was very high because of the United States' quick victory in the first Gulf War. Many observers thought he would be unbeatable in the 1992 election. Enter Bill Clinton, who focused on the economy and defeated President Bush.

In 2008, Barack Obama and John McCain ran opposite each other in the presidential election. With the low popularity of President George W. Bush and with the war dragging on in Iraq, it appeared to be a Democratic year. In spite of this, Republican McCain surged ahead after the Republican Convention and kept the poll numbers very close to Democrat Obama. Yet a few weeks before the election, the economy took a nose dive, the stock market lost more than one-third of its value, and Barack Obama won the election.

The plunging stock market created dismay and uncertainty at a crucial time. One could argue that, had the economy remained stable, it might have been a much closer race. The timing of events, whether planned or spontaneous, has a great effect on our lives.

Discerning the Right Time

Timing is everything. Comedians experience success or failure based on their ability to deliver the punch line with just the right emphasis at just the right time.

As noted, politicians can win or lose, depending on the timing of other factors in the culture prior to the time of their election.

Investment counselors try to buy when they think a stock is at its low point and sell when the stock rises to a new high. Timing is crucial in that process.

For pastors concerned about hiring staff, timing also plays an important role in achieving and maintaining momentum.

Hiring Too Soon

Pastors who hire additional staff too soon will encounter pitfalls that can have serious negative effects in the congregation.

Not being financially prepared. As we noted in the last chapter, if a pastor hires before the church is in a position to support a new staff person financially, it adds to the budgetary stress a church may already be experiencing. This will eventually force the finance committee and the board to make budget cuts, which may in turn require layoffs.

Not having the support of the leadership. If a pastor hires before church leadership fully supports the idea, criticism will likely follow soon on the heels of the new hire. Henry Ford used to say, "Don't find fault. Find a remedy." Church leaders are more inclined to help the pastor find a remedy before the fact than to help solve the problem afterward.

George Burns said, "Too bad the only people who know how to run this country are busy driving cabs and cutting hair." In

reality, others who know how to run
things are serving on boards and committees in the church, but they're often
relegated to being armchair quarter-
backs. Pastors can avoid a great deal
of criticism if they will spend the time

Too Late

I hate it in friends when they come too late to help.

—Euripides

in advance of the decision, being sure the leadership is on board
with the vision of hiring new staff.

Losing credibility. If the pastor has not earned the right to
be heard, yet moves ahead anyway, loss of credibility will follow. Tony Campolo tells about a young Christian doctor, Elias
Santana, who lives in the Dominican Republic. Turning his
back on a lucrative medical practice in Chicago, Santana
returned to his native Santo Domingo to practice medicine
among the poor.

One day, Campolo accompanied Santana when he drove
into one of the worst slums of the city. Santana worked tire-
lessly for the next few hours, diagnosing people, prescribing
cures, and helping everyone he could. After hours of ministering to people physically and medically, he honked the horn
of his truck, climbed on its roof, and began preaching the
gospel.

In the crowd Campolo noticed a young man he had met pre-
viously—one of the leaders of the Marxist student movement
on campus. Campolo went over and chided him: "Hey, Pedro!
You'd better watch out! He's going to win them all to Christ and
there will be none of them left to follow you."

The young man replied sternly, "What am I supposed to
say? Elias Santana has earned the right to be heard."[2]

A pastor is wise not to move forward in hiring new staff before earning the right to be heard. Be sure you have the support of influential opinion leaders in the congregation.

Waiting Too Long to Hire

The pastor who waits too long to hire faces a different set of problems.

Burnout of volunteers. Gordon MacDonald wrote an article in which he listed seven deadly siphons, or reasons we lose enthusiasm. One of them was "calendars without a Sabbath." He says, "A datebook filled with appointments but absent of significant hours (days) of quiet and reflection—written in first—is an abomination (an old and harsh word) to the God of the Bible, who said, 'Six days you shall labor . . . the seventh day is a Sabbath to the Lord your God.'"[3]

How sad when the pastor becomes burned out. It's even sadder when lay leaders, many of whom are already working a full-time job, become burned out because the church is slow to add professional staff. A wise pastor keeps eyes and ears open to this kind of deterioration and discerns the right time to recommend hiring new staff.

Low morale. Closely associated with burnout of volunteers is low morale. As Carisa Bianchi says, "You can always find reasons to work. There will always be one more thing to do. But when people don't take time out, they stop being productive. They stop being happy, and that affects the morale of everyone around them." When morale is high, everything seems better than it actually is. When morale is low, it can color everything with the crayon of defeat and gloom.

Loss of good candidates. When pastors delay—trying to make up their minds, trying to convince leaders and boards, trying to find the money, trying to be sure they have everything lined up to guarantee success—good candidates are slipping away to other churches that are ready to hire. While we must be prudent in planning, once we have things in place, it's time to move forward. Further delay could be costly.

> **A Fitting Reply**
>
> Everyone enjoys a fitting reply; it is wonderful to say the right thing at the right time!
>
> —Proverbs 15:23 NLT

Loss of momentum. When burnout and low morale set in, loss of momentum is sure to follow. John Mason likes to think of momentum as a large boulder at the top of a hill. If a person rocks the boulder back and forth and gets it moving, its momentum makes it almost unstoppable.[4] But if it ever does stop, especially on level ground, it takes a lot more effort to get it going again. Waiting too long to hire may well decrease momentum to a standstill. Then when you do hire, you and your new staff person have a bigger job than ever to get things moving again.

Good timing is tricky. But moving forward at the right time can keep momentum going, prevent burnout, maintain morale, and enable you to find the right person for the job.

The Importance of Timing in the Bible

There are numerous instances in the Bible where timing is a critical factor in good decision making. Even in Jesus' ministry, it's evident that he recognized the importance of timing when considering decisions and actions. We see this particularly in several statements recorded in the gospel of John:

- "'Dear woman, why do you involve me?' Jesus replied, 'My time has not yet come'" (2:4).
- "Therefore Jesus told them, 'The right time for me has not yet come; for you any time is right'" (7:6).
- "You go to the Feast. I am not yet going up to this Feast, because for me the right time has not yet come" (7:8).
- "At this they tried to seize him, but no one laid a hand on him, because his time had not yet come" (7:30).
- "It was just before the Passover Feast. Jesus knew that the time had come for him to leave this world and go to the Father. Having loved his own who were in the world, he now showed them the full extent of his love" (13:1).
- "Though I have been speaking figuratively, a time is coming when I will no longer use this kind of language but will tell you plainly about my Father" (16:25).
- "Father, the time has come. Glorify your Son, that your Son may glorify you. For you granted him authority over all people that he might give eternal life to all those you have given him" (17:2).

It's evident from these several statements, as well as many others in the Gospels, that Jesus paid careful attention to timing.

But perhaps nowhere in Scripture is the critical nature of timing, both positive and negative, more evident than in the early years of Moses' leadership.

The Consequences of Hurrying God's Timing

An adopted "prince" of Egypt, Moses was granted by God the ideal position and circumstances to advocate for the liberation of his people from the harsh bondage of Egypt. Though he had lived nearly all his life among Egyptian royalty, he still felt a strong kinship with his own tribe—the Hebrew descendants of Abraham, Isaac, and Jacob. Perhaps even in those early years, Moses began to feel a sense of calling to deliver God's people—more than forty years before his official call at the burning bush (Ex. 2–3).

One day, Moses saw one of the Hebrew slaves being harshly treated by his Egyptian master. It was too much for him to bear. He felt an overwhelming sense of responsibility and urgency to do something, rather than to allow God's people to continue to suffer at the hands of the Egyptians. Moses' urgency pushed him to act immediately—and he did, murdering the tormentor and burying his body in the sand (Ex. 2:11–12).

No one can now predict what would have happened if Moses had responded differently, if he had discerned the importance of patience and impeccable timing. How differently might the exodus have looked if Moses had resisted the temptation to take things into his own hands? No one can say. Instead, Moses was stripped of his royal standing and privilege, barely escaping with his life into a self-imposed exile. It was to be another forty years before Moses was again granted the opportunity to make good on his calling to deliver God's people from their bondage.

Second Time's a Charm

When Moses was eventually called by God to return to Egypt a second time and to demand the release of the Hebrew people from their slavery, he demonstrated the wisdom of one who has learned the lesson of timing. Once God overcame Moses' initial lack of confidence and faith, he displayed tremendous restraint and attentiveness to the timing of God's plan.

After Moses and his brother Aaron's initial meeting with Pharaoh, Pharaoh responded by dealing even more harshly with the Hebrew people (Ex. 5:1–18). Rather than again acting rashly, Moses took up his complaint with God (Ex. 5:23). A second time Moses and Aaron visited Pharaoh, and a second time they were rebuffed (Ex. 7:10–13). Still, Moses waited on God's timing.

Through several more encounters with Pharaoh—and ten remarkable and devastating signs from God—Moses remained faithful to God's plan, seeking God's will and waiting for God's timing. The result was that Moses had the opportunity to lead God's people through the defining moment in their history—the exodus from Egypt—and all because he had learned the lesson of timing.

When to Replace Volunteers with Employees

Most churches survive because they have a great host of volunteers to teach classes, care for babies, receive offerings, count money, pay bills, lead worship, staff the church kitchen, and even call on some of the sick people. Willing and competent volunteers comprise the backbone of any church.

Hired Staff versus Volunteers

But when is it time to replace volunteers with employees? As Arthur DeKruyter points out, "No one, including most church boards, wants to pay for something you can get for free."[5] So when is the time right for a church board to bite the bullet and make the decision to pay someone to do what a volunteer has done until now?

You need to hire if volunteers are approaching burnout. Growing churches tend to become more complex in their organization, so keeping track of the finances becomes a heavy responsibility for a volunteer treasurer. When your volunteer treasurer is spending twenty hours a week doing the church's books, it's not fair to him or her nor to their family obligations. The church leadership should look for a part-time bookkeeper.

You need to hire if the job requires a level of expertise that you cannot find among your volunteers. If a Sunday school has fifty students, most churches can find a volunteer leader to handle that responsibility. If a Sunday school grows to five hundred, or if the midweek children's ministry is burgeoning with hundreds of children, that's a different proposition. You will need to find a competent Christian education director who has more training, expertise, and time to give to the job than the average layperson would have.

You need to hire if volunteers are incapable of maintaining the quality of program you need. A great youth

The Supply of Time

One cannot buy, rent, or hire more time. The supply of time is totally inelastic. No matter how high the demand, the supply will not go up. There is no price for it. Time is totally perishable and cannot be stored. Yesterday's time is gone forever, and will never come back. Time is always in short supply. There is no substitute for time. Everything requires time. All work takes place in, and uses up time. Yet most people take for granted this unique, irreplaceable, and necessary resource.

—Peter F. Drucker

program cannot be built solely on the charisma of the youth pastor or leader. That works for awhile, but ultimately, a good organization needs to undergird the ministry. A dynamic children's program, with Sunday school classes, children's church for various age levels, and a midweek club program for kids requires a significant level of organization and management. A great worship experience doesn't just happen. It needs to be well planned, well staffed, and well executed. Maintaining the quality of these and other ministries requires time and expertise not available to many volunteers.

Other Timing Cues

If adequate funding is not in place, it's too soon to hire. This is a difficult place for a pastor, to see the need for professional staff, but to feel one's hands are tied because there's insufficient money in the budget to cover the cost. A friend became the pastor of a Midwestern church of 360 attendees in a university town. Approximately half the attendees were college students who, God love 'em, brought a great deal of enthusiasm and spirit to the service, but very little money. He was in the admirable position of being able to influence a generation of young adults poised to make their mark on the world. He was in the unenviable position of being unable to hire an additional pastor because the funds were not there.

He and a very efficient office secretary were the only full-time employees. My friend, who had gifts and skills of administration, needed an assistant who could do follow-up and assimilation, but they waited two years to hire such a person. During that time, the church grew by nearly one hundred attendees, competent laypeople helped in many ways, and the church budget grew to the point where they could afford a second full-time pastor. It also gave my friend time to build credibility in this congregation so the lay leadership accepted and trusted his vision for the church.

In many smaller churches, pastors utilize volunteer secretarial help until they can afford to hire a part-time secretary. In numerous churches, members alternate taking responsibility for cleaning the church on a weekly basis until they can afford to hire a part-time custodian. In thousands of churches across the country, volunteers lead the worship service until the church can afford to hire someone with expertise as a worship leader.

The Right Time

A stone thrown at the right time is better than gold given at the wrong time.

Persian proverb

If the leadership has not accepted the pastor's vision for additional staff, it's too soon to hire. Strategic thinker Aubrey Malphurs recommends three specific ways to sharpen the focus of our vision and subsequently communicate to those we're trying to convince:[6]

1. Have an accurate biblical and theological understanding of what God is calling your church to be and do. Unless you're absolutely convinced that what you envision for staff expansion aligns with Scripture and the needs of the church, your leadership will be reluctant to buy into your dream.

2. Write out planning documents that outline the specific ways you will accomplish this call in your unique setting. Fred Smith tells about working for Maxey Jarman, who would force Fred to write a memo if he sensed his thinking was fuzzy. If Fred protested that he couldn't put it in words, Maxey would

say, "The only reason you can't write it is because you don't know it. When you know it, you can write it."[7]

3. Paint a compelling picture of this vision in the minds and hearts of the people so as to catalyze them to work together to bring about God's plans for your ministry. Malphurs insists, "Visionary leaders have the capacity to see in their heads what many cannot see with the naked eye. Visionaries carry in their mental wallets a picture of what their future ministries look like."[8]

Timing Tips

Planning ahead and anticipating the future are always good exercises for the pastor who does not want to get caught by surprise. Dreaming, imagining, and envisioning are all ways to look ahead so when the time is right, you are ready to act. Consider these timing tips.

Plant Seeds

Even though you may not feel the time is right to add a staff member, you can begin to plant the seeds for such a move. Long before you are ready to hire someone, you can talk to your leaders about the need and about the pitfalls and possibilities inherent in expanding staff. Over lunch, in casual conversations, and at board meetings, you can bring up your ideas with no pressure to make a decision on the spot. If people have objections, you'll probably hear them. If they like your ideas, you will likely hear that too. Just be sure you are perceptive enough to hear the truth, and not just what you want to hear.

Think it Through

In fact, don't bring it up if you haven't thought it through. If someone else brings it up and you're not ready to discuss it intelligently, suggest that everyone give it some thought and prayer and come back together to discuss it more fully. This gives you time to do your homework. In thinking it through, you will want to consider what staff member is most needed, based on your own gifts and temperament, the needs of the church, and how deep your pool of volunteers is for any given ministry. Think about what level of training and expertise you need in that potential staff member. Think about the change in dynamics between being a solo pastor and a senior pastor.

Anticipate All the Costs

Adding staff is more expensive than you might think. If you begin with part-time personnel, the church saves a great deal of money over hiring a full-time person. Part-time employees typically earn a salary or hourly wage with no additional benefits. Full-time people usually expect health insurance,

-+>=- =<+-

A Time for Everything

There is a time for everything, and a season for every activity under heaven:

a time to be born and a time to die,

a time to plant and a time to uproot,

a time to kill and a time to heal,

a time to tear down and a time to build,

a time to weep and a time to laugh,

a time to mourn and a time to dance,

a time to scatter stones and a time to gather them,

a time to embrace and a time to refrain,

a time to search and a time to give up,

a time to keep and a time to throw away,

a time to tear and a time to mend,

a time to be silent and a time to speak,

a time to love and a time to hate,

a time for war and a time for peace.

—Ecclesiastes 3:1–8

pension, and, in the case of ministers, housing or housing allowance as well as Social Security reimbursement in whole or in part. Starting with part-time employees, whether it be secretarial or ministerial assistants, is a way for the church to expand paid staff gradually until it becomes feasible to add the benefits expected by full-time personnel.

Set Aside Funds

If you're not ready to hire staff, especially because of financial constraints, perhaps you could afford to set aside some funds in the budget toward the day when you can expand the staff. Creating a special fund in the budget would be a way to get used to the expenditure gradually while saving toward the expenses of that next staff member. Setting aside a small percentage is relatively painless at the time, yet it can provide significant funds when the time comes to hire. The savings may be used to offset the first year's expenditures or for a specific purpose, such as moving expenses.

Fine Tune Your Radar

Keep your antennae up while you're waiting for the right time to hire. Following are a few things you will need to keep on your radar:

The potential burnout of volunteers. If this is one of the signs that the church needs additional staff, you will want to be aware sooner rather than later. If at all possible, you don't want to wait until some volunteer crashes and burns before you sense the need to hire.

The quality of the ministries. If the quality of the church's ministries begins to decline, people will start shopping around for another church where they have stronger ministries for their children or youth, or a better quality of worship, or whatever the sensitive area is.

Volunteers dropping the ball. This is not the same as burnout. People have many distractions. Church involvement is just one item on their weekly agenda that likely includes children's sports, hobbies, school activities that need parental volunteers, along with heavy expectations at work. These volunteers may not be burned out as much as they are simply too busy and aren't giving their church responsibilities priority. Either way—whether it's burnout or distractions—the work of the church suffers and it may be a clue that you're getting closer to needing paid staff.

It's Finally Time!

Pastor Mark listened as his youth leader Ken recited one reason after another why he should resign. The very success they had experienced was now their downfall. Too many kids, not enough volunteers, too many complaints from the parents, not enough days in the week nor hours in a day. Ken, married with three children, worked as a computer programmer and the company he worked for expected him to put in extra hours due to the large demand on their services.

Ken stood to leave and said, "Pastor, I know we have talked about the possibility of hiring a youth pastor. I don't know if the budget will take it right now, but I think it's about time. I've done about all I can do. I have many demands at home. My wife is strapped with three preschoolers, and I need to be available to relieve her in the evenings. I think it's time for me to step aside and for the church to consider hiring a youth pastor."

Closing the door behind him, Mark sat down and reflected on what Ken had said. He couldn't blame him. The truth was that he had given faithful service, sometimes sacrificing time he should have spent with his family.

"Ken is right," Mark decided at last, and called his lay leader to set up an appointment to talk about the next steps in hiring a youth pastor. With the way the church was growing and the increased offerings lately, maybe it was time. At least they could talk about it.

Action Steps

1. Make a list of the things that will have to be in place before you hire additional staff. Include the financial costs as well as lay leadership buy-in.
2. Evaluate the burnout potential of your volunteers. Are some individuals doing too many jobs, wearing too many hats?
3. Think through the financial cost of adding staff and consider whether you may be able to begin setting aside some funds for this purpose in next year's budget.

4

PERFORMANCE
Establishing a Standard
and Job Description

*Finding the right people who will perform to your
level of expectations requires wisdom.*

Pat MacMillan remembers when his father took him on his
first fishing trip in the Cascade Mountains of Washington.
Pat was five years old. They drove for three hours before
pulling to the side of the road. His dad began rummaging in the
trunk of the car for their equipment. Meanwhile, Pat explored
the nearby terrain.

A small trickle of water at the
bottom of a graded decline caught
his attention. It looked like the
perfect place to fish. But his dad
called him in a different direction,
explaining there were no fish that close to the road. They hiked
for an hour into the foothills, passing numerous little streams.
They even passed others who were fishing in some of those
streams. Pat could see fish milling about in the quiet pools.

> Set excellent performance as
> your standard and strive to
> achieve it each day.
>
> —Brian Tracy

Finally they stopped at a small, high mountain lake. Hardly anyone else was around while they pulled in beautiful, large rainbow trout. His dad explained, "You don't find fish like these by the side of the road." They hiked back to the car in the early evening, stopping occasionally to compare catches with other fishermen. Actually, there was no comparison. The best fish were found farthest from the road.

Now, Pat makes the point that, like the fish, exceptional people are less accessible and difficult to find. Although it's hard work, it's worth it to find the exeptional instead of the acceptable.[1]

> **Earnest Effort**
>
> Whatever I have tried to do in life, I have tried with all my heart to do it well; whatever I have devoted myself to, I have devoted myself completely; in great aims and in small I have always thoroughly been in earnest.
>
> —Charles Dickens

Spotting the Snares

The question is, how does a church set a standard of performance that will attract exceptional staff people? What does a job description look like if you want to entice the best and brightest to come and work at your church?

Steve Jobs, cofounder of Apple Computers, says, "When you're in a start-up, the first ten people will determine whether the company succeeds." Gary McIntosh adapts that insight by saying, "When you're in a church, the pastoral staff will determine whether the church succeeds." Beyond that, however, he observes that hiring the first pastoral staff member is similar to choosing your child's first babysitter.

That decision affects the health, well-being, and future of the church. From that point forward, he believes, you will have to compensate for the first staff member's strengths and weaknesses.[2]

Soon after Jack Welch became CEO of General Electric, he spoke to a group of Harvard Business School students. One of them asked what was his most important task as CEO. He answered, "Choosing and developing good people."[3]

While we all agree there's no substitute for hiring the best people, what are some of the snares along the way to establishing a high standard of performance for staff?

Hiring Just to Fill a Position

Hiring a warm body to fill a slot just so you can check it off your "to do" list is a dangerous practice. As time drags on in the hiring process, you may be tempted to hire the next applicant, just to get the position filled. You will surely regret it. You want the best person you can find to achieve the church's mission. If you fail to consider whether the applicant's skills match the need, you will soon have a new staff member who is highly stressed and producing poorly.

Taking Shortcuts

It usually takes time to find the right person. Peter Drucker observed, "People decisions are time-consuming for the simple reason that the Lord did not create people as resources for the organization. They do not come in the proper size or shape for the tasks to be done in the organization—and they cannot be machined down or recast for these tasks."[4]

MacMillan warns that often "shortcuts lead to a dead end. Those that tend to 'wing it' on the front end often 'crash and burn' on the back end."[5]

Talking Too Much and Listening Too Little

You may be tempted to impress the candidate by telling him or her about the church, about your philosophy of ministry, and about the potential in the community. You can share all these things in due time. But you want to hear what the candidate has to say. If you ask a question and simply listen, candidates will often tell you more than they ever intended to say. If you find yourself talking a great deal, remember the acronym WAIT, which represents, "Why Am I Talking?" Remind yourself to "zip it," ask a question, and let the interviewee talk.

Showing the Full Job Description Too Soon

Closely related to talking too much is revealing too much about the job. When you lay out the complete job description too soon, candidates will tend to portray themselves in terms of what they have just read. Either consciously or unconsciously, they will tell you what you want to hear. Describe the job with broad brush strokes, and focus on learning about the candidate. You can always share the details later.

Hiring a Superstar

Avoid the person who has done it all and had the greatest success. This may sound contradictory to the idea that you want to hire the best people. However, superstars are often not very good team players. They're often more concerned with their individual success than they are with your church's vision and mission. They're also prone to flame out and leave prematurely. Then you will have to pick up the pieces when people who learned to love and trust the new staff member are left high and dry.

Hiring the Least Experienced Person

The flip side of the coin is this: don't hire the least experienced person, especially if the reason is you feel you cannot afford someone who is better qualified. Wait until you can assemble the finances to afford a more experienced person. In the long run, you'll regret having hired someone who actually becomes a project. In other words, as senior pastor, if you hire such a person, you may have to spend an excessive amount of time training, molding, and shaping that individual. A more experienced person, especially a self-starter, would be off and running without so much supervision.

The Right Person

If you have the right executives on the bus, they'll do everything within their power to build a great company, not because of what they will "get" for it, but because they simply cannot imagine settling for anything less.

—Jim Collins

The Person Whom God Chooses

When God needed someone to carry out an assignment, he found the best person available at the time. Had we known those individuals, we might have questioned some of his choices. Gideon himself wondered why God chose him as he trembled and threshed wheat in a winepress, hoping to hide it from the dreaded Midianites. He viewed himself as the weakest member of the weakest clan of Israel (Judg. 6:1–15).

Jeremiah protested he was only a child and did not know how to speak when God called him to be a prophet. But God strengthened him to be like "a fortified city, an iron pillar and a bronze wall" in order to declare God's message (Jer. 1:4–18).

Asaph wrote a psalm in which he described David's qualifications to be God's man. He inscribed the fact that God "chose David his servant and took him from the sheep pens; from tending the sheep he brought him to be the shepherd of his people Jacob, of Israel his inheritance. And David shepherded them with integrity of heart; with skillful hands he led them" (Ps. 78:70–72).

Before David was a leader, he was a servant. This youngest son of Jesse served in a remote place. Apparently God knew that David's shepherd heart would serve him well when given the opportunity to shepherd his people Israel. In fact, Peter declares that pastors should be "shepherds of God's flock . . . not lording it over those entrusted to you, but being examples to the flock" (1 Pet. 5:2–3).

A Person of Character

David also led Israel with integrity, which is a Hebrew word meaning "soundness," "simplicity," and "uprightness."[6] Another word for *integrity* is *character*, which comes from a Greek word meaning *chisel*. We don't possess character as a natural trait from birth, like fingerprints. We have to chisel character out of the raw materials God gives us, along with the circumstances life throws at us.

Bill Hybels says, "When searching for someone to add to a volunteer team or a paid staff position, I remind myself, *Character first*. By this I mean that I need to have confidence in a person's walk with Jesus Christ. . . . I need to see evidence of honesty, teachability, humility, reliability, a healthy work ethic, and a willingness to be entreated."[7]

What is the applicant like as a person? Apart from professional gifts and status, apart from intellectual capabilities, what kind of person is he or she? This speaks to the matter of character. Peter Drucker, the management guru, said, "By themselves, character and integrity do not accomplish anything. But their absence faults everything else."[8]

A Person of Competence

David also led Israel with skill. "With skillful hands he led them," says the writer (Ps. 78:72). This speaks to us about competence. In other words, be cautious about hiring anyone who is untested. Someone with a few years' experience will serve you and the church better than a novice.

Drucker warned, "If you find someone whose qualifications look good, but he or she is unhappy or unemployed, be very cautious. The kind of people you are looking for are probably making huge contributions and setting records somewhere. They are probably deliriously happy and

> **People Are Remarkable**
>
> Humans can turn nothing into something, pennies into fortune, and disaster into success. And the reason they can do such remarkable things is because they are remarkable. Try reaching down inside of yourself; you'll come up with some more of those remarkable human gifts. They're there, waiting to be discovered and employed.
>
> —Jim Rohn

much loved by the people they work with. Go after that type. Go after proven competence."[9]

A Person of Compatibility

Besides character and competence, we need people who are compatible. How do they fit into the church? Do they complement the gifts of the senior pastor? A pastor who has excellent skills at connecting with new people and leading persons to Christ may need an assistant who excels at administration. How does the prospective new hire fit with the mix of people in the congregation? Is the congregation blue collar or white collar? Suburban or inner city? If the new person comes from a radically different background, can he or she adapt?

Ken Blanchard advised an employer never to hire a person who doesn't have a positive emotional effect on the interviewer the minute he or she walks into the room.[10] This could be called chemistry as well as compatibility. But the connection must be more than a good feeling. Is the person really a good fit?

Qualities for Performance

Character
Competence
Compatibility

The diagram to the left shows three overlapping circles. Each overlaps the other two and all three interlock at one point. Each circle also has an area that overlaps neither of the others and is unique to that circle alone. The graphic demonstrates the various ways the three qualities may be present or absent in a candidate.

If a candidate has only one factor going for him or her, whether it's character, competence, or compatibility, do not hire that person. Look further; someone else is better qualified.

If a candidate has both competence and compatibility but is weak in character, do not hire that person. You might develop skills, but it's extremely difficult to develop integrity in adults who are already afflicted with character flaws.

A person of high integrity and good compatibility may be a good hire if he or she is very sharp and capable. You may be able to provide skills on the job.

If a candidate has good character and competence but doesn't fit, it's inadvisable to hire the person. Look for someone who is more compatible.

When you find a candidate who resides in that small area where all three circles overlap, he or she is your best option.

Seeking Peak Performers

If peak performers were easy to find, every church would have lots of them. By definition, those who truly excel are in the minority. Specifically, what should we be looking for? What qualities are we likely to find in high achievers?

Hire Equippers

When pastors hire their first staff person, they're tempted to find a congenial, well-trained, hard-working individual who will do the work of three or four people. We hope to find someone highly skilled in ministry. Your goal is to get as much productivity out of this person as possible. Yet what we really need is to find those who will train others. In other words, hire workers that are also *equippers*.

A person who can train others to do the work of the ministry, as Paul indicates in Ephesians 4, will multiply his or her effectiveness. This is not an attempt to dodge work or dump it on someone else. It's a well-planned strategy to maximize effectiveness and incorporate more people in the ministry.

Alan Nelson describes a trend toward team ministry in which staff pastors will "learn new skills and . . . become coaches instead of 'tellers' and developers instead of doers. . . . Talent will be replaced with team-building skills as a staff hiring priority."[11]

Look for Racehorses

Having clarified that the goal is to hire equippers, then look for the best person you can find. "Racehorses are creative people who do not know what it means to say something cannot be done. Many times they will drive leaders crazy but they get up early, stay up late, and most important, get things done!"[12] In contrast to a racehorse, a mule tends to play by the rules and does quite well where the work is fairly standardized and no extra effort is required. You have to prod a mule, but racehorses are, well, off to the races! In other words, you are looking for self-starters.

Beware of Clock-Watchers

These underachievers put in the minimum of time and effort. Their favorite times of the workday are lunch and quitting time. They're the people about whom the wag was talking when he said, "If you don't believe in the resurrection of the dead, you should be around here at quitting time!"

It's another way of saying you want to find people of passion. When Magic Johnson entered the NBA after his sophomore year in college, he joined a group of veteran players on the Los Angeles Lakers. In his first season as a pro, Johnson watched Kareem Abdul Jabbar make a basket at the buzzer to send a game into overtime. In his enthusiasm, Magic tackled Jabbar as the veteran walked off the floor, nearly wrestling him to the ground.

> **Be the Best You Can Be**
>
> If a man is called to be a street sweeper, he should sweep streets even as Michelangelo painted, or Beethoven composed music, or Shakespeare wrote poetry. He should sweep streets so well that all the hosts of heaven and earth will pause and say, here lived a great street sweeper who did his job well.
>
> —Martin Luther King, Jr.

Jabbar shook him off and said, "Hey, rookie, it's a 72 game season. Keep your cool, man."

But Lakers coach Pat Riley said Magic never did keep his cool. His passion for the game of basketball ignited the entire team and they won the NBA championship that year, led by the nineteen-year-old Johnson.[13]

That's the kind of person you're looking for—minus the tackling, of course.

Seek Long-term Relationships

You may hire a person who eventually becomes a senior pastor himself. If that happens, you celebrate their new ministry and send them out with your blessing. But if you can find someone who has no such ambition, but rather desires to work alongside a senior pastor in a supportive role, focusing on a particular ministry that expands the kingdom, you are a blessed senior pastor.

Having said that, be open to the idea of bringing in a potential senior pastor, spend some time training and mentoring, and then send him out to plant a church. Blessed is the senior pastor who can send a protégé into a church-planting situation along with some people from the mother church in order the multiply the kingdom with a new daughter congregation.

Don't Confuse Aggressiveness with Initiative

Good leaders come in many shapes and sizes, different styles and temperaments. Some are quiet and lead by example. Others are more assertive and are obviously front-runners. Others who are extremely effective work best behind the scenes.

What you want to find in a prospective staff person is initiative, not necessarily aggressiveness. As Don Cousins points out, "An initiator takes action, but unlike the purely aggressive person, he does it for others' sake rather than his own."[14] Cousins goes on to observe that aggressive and hard-working businessmen might seem like good leadership candidates on the surface. But only when they submit to the Holy Spirit and accountability with other leaders do they have a chance of becoming effective, godly leaders.

Putting Together a Job Description

Anyone who applies for a position with your church deserves to have a detailed job description that will clarify expectations.

I have seen position descriptions that were so sketchy and general that applicants would have little guidance as to what was expected. What are some things a job description should include?

Define Qualifications

Before describing all the responsibilities of the position, list a few bullet points about qualifications. Some of these will state the obvious. One job description states: "The assistant pastor must be a born-again, Spirit-filled individual, who senses the call of God to full-time Christian work." It may seem ludicrous to specify what "everybody knows" as the basic qualifications of the job. But is it?

A denominational supervisor told me about an ambitious lay leader in one church who called him and said he had downloaded eighteen resumes from the Internet. Would it be okay to distribute those to his board for consideration? The shocked supervisor told the lay leader to send them to him first so he could screen them. The resumes came from individuals who hailed from a variety of denominational and theological backgrounds, some of whom were obviously not suited for the open position. A job description that states the qualifications helps to clarify the kind of individual for whom the church is looking.

You may want to specify that you want a person from a specific theological persuasion. If you expect the person to have certain competencies, such as a skill in leading others to Christ one-on-one, it's helpful to state it. Do you expect the person to be ordained or pursuing ordination? Do you expect a certain educational level? This is the place to clarify all such qualifications. In other words, what kind of person do you want this applicant to be?

List Responsibilities

This is the place to specify exactly what you want this person to do. If you're hiring a youth pastor or pastor of student ministries, what age groups will he or she oversee? Junior high students? Senior high? College students? Be specific.

A Person of Value

Try not to become a success, but rather try to become a man of value.

—Albert Einstein

How will this person relate to adult youth sponsors? How often will they meet? Are there teaching responsibilities connected with this job or only supervisory expectations? Will this person become pastor over an age group and relate to them in a pastoral way—visitation, counseling directly with the individuals, directing group activities—or does this person manage the ministry through others? State what you expect.

You may want to hire a person to oversee more than one area. Perhaps you're looking for someone to supervise youth and worship arts or to oversee spiritual formation and student ministries. Define these responsibilities as specifically as you can. If you expect the applicant to spend 60 percent of his or her time in one area and 40 percent in another, state that up front.

Clarify Accountability

To whom will this person report? How often? What about staff meetings? How frequently will they occur? Is attendance compulsory? Does the individual have any reporting responsibilities to the church's ruling body, the board, or the elders? Clarify these matters early in the relationship. The job description itself is a good place to show it.

A pastor friend told me he once assumed a pastorate where the board had bypassed the former senior pastor to reprimand a staff person. In his denomination, the senior pastor has clear responsibilities for supervising staff. So as they approached the time for hiring a new assistant pastor, the senior minister asked the board a question:

"As we consider hiring a new assistant, I assume you would not approve of such a person doing an end run around the pastor to get to the board with his or her concerns. Am I correct?"

The board verified that would be inappropriate.

"By the same token," the senior pastor continued, "I think it would be inappropriate for you as a board to do an end run around me to deal with my staff." As the board did a double-take, he added, "If I am doing my job as the supervisor of staff, that should never be necessary and I want you to know I take such responsibilities very seriously."

By clarifying who was accountable to whom, he avoided a potential conflict down the road. It never became a problem.

Specify Compensation

When I say "specify compensation," I do not mean you list the exact salary on the job description. You may not want to be that specific that early in the relationship.

But you can list the fact that there is a salary plus benefits and specify what the benefits are. For instance, the applicant has a right to know the church's policy about such things as

- vacation time,
- sick leave,
- health insurance benefits,
- pension payments,
- whether Social Security is reimbursed, in the case of ministerial staff, or
- reimbursed expenses to attend conferences.

If you're hiring someone for a salaried position, what is the level of performance you expect of that individual? While not specifying the number of hours, you may want to clarify, for instance, that you want them to be at work by 8:00 a.m. and stay at least until 4:30 p.m., if that's the church's expectation. If you expect them to divide their time between office work and visitation, other contacts, or projects, you should specify this.

Finding Superior Performers

Pastor Glen closed the door after young Jim left his office. Returning to his desk, Glen sat down and reflected on the interview. Jim had applied for the position of assistant pastor and Glen had granted the interview as a favor to a neighboring pastor who gave Jim a positive recommendation. It was obvious to Glen that Jim's work ethic left much to be desired. The young minister asked many questions about vacation time, days off, and flex time for working at home instead of keeping regular office hours. Glen could anticipate a disaster in the making. It was almost as if the young man were more interested in what the church could do for him than in the quality of work he could perform on behalf of God and the church.

Management expert Robert Townsend said, "Leaders come in all sizes, ages, shapes, and conditions. Some are poor administrators, some are not overly bright. But there is one clue for spotting them. Since most people *per se* are mediocre, the true leader can be recognized because somehow or other, his people consistently turn in superior performances."[15]

The old adage is true: "The best predictor of future performance is past performance." Some people whine at that statement and declare that faithfulness is more important than performance. In reality, we need both. The person who is faithful will perform. We all have bad years or bad experiences when performance doesn't rise to our level of expectation. But eventually faithfulness will lead us to perform well.

> **The Habit of Excellence**
> We are what we repeatedly do. Excellence, then, is not an act but a habit.
> —Aristotle

As you establish a standard of performance for your church and staff, be as specific as you can with your job descriptions, be thorough in your reference-checking, and you'll find some applicants who love God, love people, have a great work ethic, and will meet your performance standards.

Action Steps

1. List the nonnegotiable qualities you're looking for in your next staff person.
2. Discuss with your lay leaders their expectations for the next staff person.
3. Devise a job description that includes qualifications, responsibilities, lines of accountability, and compensation.

5

ASSESSMENT
Conducting the Interview

*A senior pastor who wants to hire the best people will
become skillful in the art of interviewing.*

When Pastor Tim opened the door to welcome the applicant
for youth pastor, he was mildly shocked, although he
tried not to let his face betray his surprise. The young man was
wearing a baggy T-shirt, shorts, and sandals, while his wife
wore a tank top. Yes, it was a hot,
humid day in June. And yes,
he heard the apologies for their
appearance; the air conditioner
quit working in their old car that
had barely made it to the church.
A recent seminary graduate, he
told the senior pastor the jalopy
had gotten them through school but was now near death.

> Although it's too often
> overworked, the interview
> is a primary source of
> information and critically
> important in the evaluation
> process.
>
> —Pat MacMillan

"Boy, it sure feels nice and cool in here," his young wife said,
sinking into a chair next to her husband and opposite the pastor.

The interview went well, once the pastor got past the shock of their initial appearance. He had reviewed the résumé just before they arrived and had prepared two pages of potential questions. They would meet the church board later that evening and would tour the city the next day before interacting with the youth group at an informal get-together.

The young man was forthcoming in the interview, seemingly honest in his answers, and humble in realizing he lacked experience, although he had served a couple of youth ministry internships while in seminary. His wife seemed supportive of their ministry. In addition to youth ministry, the job description called for him to assume some assistant pastor duties as well, at the discretion of the senior pastor. He seemed eager to learn, passionate about working with youth, and anxious to get started.

Common Interviewing Mistakes

Interviews are the major way senior pastors get to know their applicants, although they have four sources of information about a candidate for a staff position:

- résumé
- interview
- references
- testing

Later in this chapter, we'll discuss these four in more detail, but in this section I want to address the interview.

An analyst estimated that American businesses spent approx-imately twenty-six billion dollars in managerial time preparing for and conducting interviews in 1987.[1] That's an old statistic, so my guess is, if anything, the amount is larger now. MacMillan goes on to point out that interviewers with no training have a 22 per-cent chance of predicting job success, while training doubles the success rate to 44 percent.[2] Even so, this is less than a fifty-fifty chance of getting it right, based strictly on the interview. So we must think in terms of a balanced approach.

Interviewing is still a vital part of hiring the right person for the job. But for now, let's look at some what can go wrong with the interview process.

+≻══ ══≺+

Judging People

Nearly all of us believe that we are above average in our sense of humor, our ability to drive and to judge people. It's the last of these that gets us into trouble with hiring.

—Dale Dauten

Asking Shallow Questions

Closed questions, the kind that can be answered with a simple yes or no, will not give the interviewer the kind of information he or she needs. Neither will asking questions for which the answer is obvious. For instance, if an interviewer asks an applicant about strengths and weaknesses, the person in the hot seat is going to recite mostly strengths, while creatively trying "to explain why he or she can't think of any weaknesses and sound sincere at the same time."[3]

Even if you ask open-ended questions requiring an essay type of answer, people may still give short, shallow responses. In this case, you simply have to ask for more information. "Cindy, tell me more . . ." or "Jim, can you give me an example . . . ?"

Taking Inadequate Notes

While you don't want to unnerve the applicant by rabid note-taking, especially if he or she has just revealed a weakness, at the same time you likely don't have perfect recall. Taking simple notes that you can elaborate on later will help you recall important facts and impressions about the candidate. I suggest you write out your questions in advance, leaving a space to jot down the answers as the applicant gives them.

Poor Listening

Many interviewers make the mistake of talking too much and listening too little. It's easy to be enthusiastic about your church, about your people, and about the opportunity you're offering. It's easy to go overboard in trying to convince applicants that your church would be the ideal place for them.

However, the purpose of the interview is to learn more information about the applicant. This is your opportunity to get acquainted. Certainly part of that process is the applicant getting acquainted with you and the church, but talking too much leaves inadequate room for their answers.

As you exult about your situation, you may inadvertently give too many answers to the applicant. If applicants listen carefully, they will pick up on what you're looking for, the qualities you're seeking, and the kind of person you think will fit. This enables them to give the answers you want to hear rather than

Let the Candidate Talk First

When you hire a staff member, you are often making a multiyear decision about someone you may talk to for only a few hours. So let the candidate talk first.

—Gary L. McIntosh

81

the truth. I'm not suggesting your applicants are dishonest. I'm suggesting they're human enough to portray themselves as fitting the mold if you're too transparent about what the ideal looks like.

A good rule of thumb is to talk 20 percent of the time and listen 80 percent.

Jumping to Conclusions

Wayne Cascio revealed that one of the most extensive research projects on how people select employees showed that "the typical interviewer reaches his or her conclusion within the first four minutes of the interview."[4]

Making Personnel Decisions

Among the effective executives I have had occasion to observe, they have been people who make decisions fast, and people who make them slowly. But without exception they make personnel decisions slowly and they make them several times before they really commit themselves.

—Peter Drucker

This kind of rapid response to a candidate is based more on charisma than on character, more on appearance than on aptitude, and more on their approach than on their answers. How can anyone know whether a person is a good fit for a job in four minutes? Yet in our humanness, we often make snap judgments that may or may not be accurate.

If the interview alone is not enough to determine whether a person should be hired (remember the other sources—resume, references, testing), how could we possibly make a valid decision in less than five minutes? Avoid jumping to conclusions.

Asking Applicants to Comment on Their Own Character

The interviewer is biased in favor of his or her own church. But we must remember that a candidate is biased in favor of him- or herself. If you ask, "Are you a person of good character?" or "Are you a person of solid integrity?" what do you think the candidate will say? "No, I'm a person who totally lacks integrity!" Hardly.

Character traits are best discovered in reference-checking. Here you can ask questions about character to an impartial third party who has knowledge of the applicant.

Interviewing for the Office of King

The prophet stepped out with fear and trembling as he made his way to Bethlehem. If King Saul should hear that Samuel was searching for a new king, the monarch would bring the prophet's career to a quick and untimely end. But God had determined Saul's days were numbered. The king had disobeyed the Lord in various ways. So in obedience to the Lord, Samuel went in spite of his fear and arrived at the city gates.

When the elders of the city saw him, they engaged in more fear and trembling. The reputation of this prophet had preceded him. Awe filled the elders as they wondered why the man of God would show up in their humble city. They asked if he came in peace. When Samuel assured them he had, they breathed a sigh of relief.

"I have come to sacrifice to the LORD," he told them. "Consecrate yourselves and come to the sacrifice with me" (1 Sam. 16:5). He also invited Jesse and his sons to the sacrifice, again following the Lord's instructions.

Looking for the Best Candidate

God had told him only that one of Jesse's sons would be the new king and that the Lord would show him which one. When Eliab, the eldest, came forward, Samuel assumed he was the one. "Surely the Lord's anointed stands here before the Lord," Samuel thought.

But God corrected his premature judgment by saying, "Do not consider his appearance or his height, for I have rejected him. The LORD does not look at the things man looks at. Man looks at the outward appearance, but the LORD looks at the heart" (1 Sam. 16:7).

As each of Jesse's other sons passed by him, Samuel rejected them, declining seven in all. Finally, he asked Jesse if he had any other sons, to which Jesse answered, "There is still the youngest, but he is tending the sheep" (1 Sam. 16:11). Samuel told Jesse to call for David to come. They would not sit down until this youngest son arrived.

When David came in, the Lord assured Samuel he should anoint young David as king. David too was impressive-looking, "ruddy, with a fine appearance and handsome features" (1 Sam. 16:12). But this is not why God told Samuel to anoint him.

Finding a Person with a Heart for God

Earlier, Samuel had confronted Saul with this message: "But now your kingdom will not endure; the LORD has sought out a man *after his own heart* and appointed him leader of his people, because you have not kept the LORD's command" (1 Sam. 13:14, emphasis added).

When Samuel began looking at Jesse's sons, the Lord cautioned him not to be swayed by the "outward appearance" because "the LORD looks at the heart" (1 Sam. 16:7). Centuries later, Paul gave the people of Pisidian Antioch a lesson in Jewish history. He reminded them that after rejecting Saul as king, the Lord said, "'I have found David son of Jesse a man after my own heart; he will do everything I want him to do" (Acts 13:22).

Samuel's anointing of David as the next king bears no exact parallel to our own process of interviewing candidates. Yet it does remind us that in the work of the Lord, we dare not overlook the condition of a person's heart. Outward appearances are deceiving. Kenneth Chafin reminds us that "we live in a world where physical beauty outranks spiritual depth, where success in business and in church tends to be defined in materialistic terms, and where charisma is prized above character."[5]

Through all means possible, we must do our best to discover the condition of a candidate's heart. How fortunate if you find a person who is not only of good character, but one who truly has a heart for God, his people, and his work.

The wise man observed, "The purposes of a man's heart are deep waters, but a man of understanding draws them out" (Prov. 20:5). Interviewers would do well to pray for understanding as they ask questions of their applicants.

Seeking Persons of Character

Character qualities rose to the top of the apostles' expectations for lay leaders in the early church. They instructed the believers to "choose seven men from among you who are known to be full of the Spirit and wisdom" (Acts 6:3). Stephen was one of the seven and the writer describes him specifically as "a man full of faith and of the Holy Spirit" (Acts 6:5).

Jesus was a master at asking pertinent questions. "Can you drink the cup I am going to drink?" He asked James and John. On another occasion, he asked the disciples, "Who do people say I am?" And more personally, he asked, "But what about you? Who do you say I am?"

By asking these searching questions, he penetrated the surface and stimulated their thinking. With God's help, we too can ask penetrating questions of our applicants. Our goal is not to make them uncomfortable, but to stimulate their thinking and to move beyond superficial answers.

Using All Sources of Information Wisely

A typical pattern for finding information about job applicants is as follows:

- Collect resumes.
- Sift the resumes, discarding those that are obviously not a good fit by whatever criteria makes sense in your situation.
- Call the top three or four candidates and interview them on the phone.
- Place an initial call to a reference or two, preferably the individual's immediate supervisor.
- Invite the candidate of your choice for an on-site interview.
- Do further reference checking, particularly to explore any areas of uncertainty.

- Conduct testing, if any.
- Conduct final interview, if needed, prior to hiring.

I mentioned earlier the four sources of information about an applicant—resumes, interviews, references, and testing. Let's look at each in more detail.

Résumés

One of the pitfalls many pastors fall into when searching for a new staff member is to rely too heavily on the resume. Resumes can fool you. Everybody tries to look good on his or her resume. Why wouldn't you put your best foot forward when you're trying to land a job?

The resume alone is not foolproof, which is why you need other means of verifying information and getting to know the applicant better. A friend told me an applicant with very little experience sent him a résumé and, on the surface, there was nothing outstanding about it. But the applicant followed up with a telephone call. Hearing his voice on the phone and sensing his enthusiasm for ministry made all the difference in my friend's attitude toward the applicant.

Most resumes are chronological. That is, they give you the applicant's job history, typically in order from the most recent to the most distant. This is helpful because it shows you how long they served at each place. When applicants switch jobs every couple of years, it's a signal and you need to discover why they changed frequently. Sometimes there are good reasons; sometimes it alerts you to a person's restlessness, inability to get along well with others, or some other difficult conditions.

You may see a resume now and then that is functional. In other words, it describes the applicant's skills. It may include information under categories such as leadership, management, supervision, training, or people skills. This type of resume isn't as helpful, because it doesn't specify where the person worked, for how long, and under what circumstances.

Some churches use an application form in addition to the resume because they are looking for certain traits in their applicants. On an application form, you can ask questions every candidate has to answer, which gives you a basis of comparison.

Résumés usually contain information about a person's educational background. This is helpful, but beware: It tells you only where they went to school and perhaps what curriculum they studied. It does not tell you what or how much they learned.

You will need to probe for additional information if the applicants use certain words on their resumes. If they say they "contributed to" some kind of task, what does that mean? Did they stand on the sidelines and offer casual suggestions, or were they integrally involved in the process. Big difference.

If they say they "organized" some project, specifically what does that mean? MacMillan suggests you watch out for the *ate* words, like *coordinate, orchestrate, facilitate, initiate, generate.*[6] These words are too general and you'll want to probe for more information.

Interviews

Of the four sources of information, more people rely on the interview than any of the other three. A good interview really provides you with an inner view of the candidate.[7]

One of the secrets of a good interview involves good preparation. Reviewing the resume before the applicant comes in and writing out pertinent questions in advance are two ways to prepare for an interview.

Once the candidate sits down, establishing good rapport, active listening, probing further when an applicant doesn't give enough information, and treating the candidate with courtesy are a few of the ways you can ensure the interview accomplishes its purpose.

Some churches with large staffs will also use group interviews to determine if the applicant is a good fit with the rest of the team. Even if this is your first addition to the staff, you may want to invite a wise and trusted layperson to participate in part of the interview. Be sure that person has a vision for ministry similar to the senior pastor's, knows the job description, and is favorable toward the staff expansion.

References

Reference checking enables you to find out how applicants have performed earlier in their career.

I'm amazed when I hear about pastors who hire staff people without checking references. I've known denominational supervisors who say a pastor will sometimes accept an appointment at another church and no one from the new church contacted the supervisor to ask any questions about the departing pastor. Why wouldn't people want to know what the immediate supervisor thought of the pastor's performance?

In the case of staff personnel, the denominational supervisor might or might not have pertinent knowledge of the individual,

⊰━ ━⊱

Before Hiring

Four questions to ask before hiring:

1. What will this person do to be liked? It's nice to be liked, but as a leader it can't be the controlling factor.
2. Does this person have a destructive weakness? A destructive weakness may not show up on a test; it's a character flaw.
3. Can this person accept reasonable mistakes? Failure is part of accepting leadership; you can't let it eat away at you.
4. Can I provide this person the environment to succeed? It's so important, particularly in the early days of someone's leadership, that he or she be put into a congenial environment.

—adapted from Fred Smith

since the senior pastor has immediate supervision over staff. But by all means, contact the senior pastor and see what he has to say about a prospective new hire.

Testing

Some people think tests—personality profiles, psychological inventories, temperament analyses—are the answer. They think tests are the ultimate reliability measurement since they are objective and not subject to the biases of an interviewer.

Others have little to do with tests, don't trust them, and see them as useful only to those who won't take the time to do interviews. They would rather trust their own instincts, intuition, and judgment of character than to rely on a cold, impersonal test.

What we must remember is that testing is one of four sources. None of the four is the total answer. A well-rounded evaluation will use more than one and perhaps all four methods. Psychologists have available to them more than a thousand accepted tests that measure a tremendous array of human traits.[8] Some tests are so complex that they must be sent off to a third party to be scored and evaluated. Other tests are the type that pastors with training can administer and score themselves.

MacMillan recommends that because tests can be expensive and time-consuming, they be used in certain situations:

- If the position in question is high-level and a mistake in hiring could be very costly.
- If a mistake in hiring would result in great emotional and/or financial cost to the candidate and his or her family. For instance, missionaries considering overseas service.
- If a candidate seems to have good potential, but some sources have waved warning signs.[9]

Making the Most of Reference Checking

Because reference checking is a valuable source of information about applicants, I'm devoting more space to it in this chapter.

Reference checking can be extremely revealing. Or frustrating. Most people you call about a prospective staff person will be honest with you. Occasionally you will find someone who is not willing to be forthcoming with information. That alone should tell you something. Either the candidate didn't have a good experience at the place in question or perhaps the candidate and the reference didn't have a good relationship. Either piece of information can be helpful to you.

Some people will be guarded, even creative, in their comments, like these recommendations mentioned by Robert Thornton, a professor at Lehigh University. Note the tongue-in-cheek aspect and the double meanings in several of the statements:

- To describe a candidate who is inept: "I most enthusias-tically recommend this candidate with no qualifications whatsoever."
- To describe a candidate who is not industrious: "In my opinion you will be very fortunate to get this person to work for you."
- To describe someone who is not worth a second look: "I would urge you to waste no time in making this candidate an offer of employment."
- To describe a person with less-than-stellar credentials: "All in all, I cannot say enough good things about this candidate or recommend him too highly."
- To describe a person who had difficulty getting along with others: "I am pleased to say that this candidate is a former colleague of mine."
- To describe an unproductive person: "I can assure you that no person would be better for this job."

Reference checking can be done in various ways, such as by e-mail, telephone, letter, or in person. Few use letters anymore because it takes too long. In-person interviews are helpful, if a reference lives nearby. Telephone interviews have the advantage of being less time-consuming and allowing the interviewer to sense something of the reference's feelings and attitudes about the applicant.

Consider these twelve points, adapted from a seminar Dr. David McKenna conducted on reference checking:

1. It's better to "spend a nickel" in reference checking than to spend big bucks on the other end by making a mistake in your selection.

2. Most *recent* past performance is the very best predictor of future performance.

3. The GAG Principle: prospective leaders grow by Going Against the Grain. If everything comes up positive in the first round of reference checking, keep looking.

4. You must be willing to ask tough questions even if the candidate is a wonderful Christian.

5. The key functions of reference checking are to reveal character, clarify competence, and confirm credentials.

6. Ask the reference for secondary reference (those not provided by the candidate him- or herself). The opinions of secondary references are often more important to consider than primary references.

7. Consider a 360 approach, that is, talking to the candidate's superiors, equals/colleagues, and subordinates.

8. Don't let a candidate's failure in the past immediately cancel out that candidate. Try to find out what they learned from failure. Did they repeat it? Did they change?

9. Assure confidentiality. The reference person you are interviewing must be secure about this.

10. Listen for clues, such as hesitation or pause in answering a question.

11. Be courteous and don't take too much of your interviewee's time; twenty to twenty-five minutes maximum.

12. Write a report or expand on your notes immediately after the interview.[10]

If applicants are fresh out of college and looking for their first full-time ministry assignment, they're likely to list friends and college professors as references. When you talk to professors, be sure you find out more than what kind of students the applicants were or what kind of grades they made. Find out something about their submission to the discipline of education, their integrity (no cheating, no plagiarism), and their temperament (moody, cheerful, belligerent). A glowing first impression may dim in the light of a serious talk with a mentor or professor. Likewise a moderate first impression may brighten after the helpful insight of one who knew the applicant in previous circumstances.

+>→ →<+

The Guidance of the Holy Spirit

The Holy Spirit is committed to being your guide. (See John 16:13.) The pathways of ministry are dotted with the walking wounded who have ignored the still, small voice of the Spirit and listened to the crowd. What took early church leaders forty days of prayer and fasting to decide, modern leaders often settle in forty seconds!

Regardless of the method you use—resume, interview, references, testing—rely on the Holy Spirit for wisdom and guidance. When the apostles were in the Upper Room following the ascension of Jesus, they decided to choose someone to replace Judas Iscariot. "So they proposed two men: Joseph called Barsabbas (also known as Justus) and Matthias. Then they prayed" (Acts 1:23–24).

Don't make your final decision about an applicant unless you've prayed. In fact, don't make any important decision without seeking the guidance of the Holy Spirit.

CONDUCTING THE INTERVIEW

Getting Beyond Appearance

After Pastor Tim concluded the interview with the applicant for the youth pastor position, he was more impressed than he had been upon first appearances. He felt the young man had a lot to learn about appropriate dress in an interview and perhaps about what's appropriate in some other ways. But he had to admit, he liked the guy. His passion and enthusiasm for ministry were contagious.

The meeting with the board went well (the young man and his wife changed to appropriate business casual attire). In the days that followed, Pastor Tim called four references, all of whom had very positive things to say about the young candidate. He had been an outstanding student at seminary, a leader among his peers, highly respected for his integrity, and admired for his passion.

Pastor Tim spent some time in prayer and then decided that as long as the personality inventory he had asked the young man and his wife to take showed no major glitches, he would hire him. He began to look forward to their new relationship.

Action Steps

1. Think about the last time you interviewed an applicant. What went well? What do you wish you had done differently? What did you learn?
2. What other questions would you ask?

6

RETENTION
Holding on to Quality Staff

*A senior pastor is only as strong as the people
he can bring around him and retain.*

Pastor Daniel walked out of the senior pastor's office, turned, and trudged down the hall to his own office. He went inside and shut the door. Sitting down at the desk, he sighed and stared into space for several long minutes. His feelings ran the gamut from hurt to anger.

Mrs. Gibson had been at it again. This time she convinced Pastor Sam, the senior pastor, that Daniel was ineffective as a youth pastor.

When it comes to staff climate and maturation, the senior minister functions either like a channel through which attitudes and resources flow, or like a cork in a bottle that restricts the flow.

—Norman Shawchuck[1]

"Have you seen his office?" she fumed. "It's a royal mess. I don't know how he can find his desk with all the books and papers piled up like that. He is so unorganized."

When Sam called Daniel into his office, he pointed out what Mrs. Gibson had said.

"Did she give specific examples of how I'm not effective?" he asked his supervisor.

"Well, no," Sam admitted, "but your disorganized office is a signal to her that you're not doing a good job."

"Pastor, I'm the first to admit that I'm not well organized when it comes to keeping a tidy office. But the youth group is growing. Three new kids received Christ last week. We had a record attendance at the recent retreat. I think things are better than ever."

"Yes, but in Mrs. Gibson's mind, you're lazy."

"But, Pastor, you know that's not true."

"Yes, I do, but in her mind, her perception is reality."

"Can't you convince her otherwise?"

"Dan, you know how influential she is in this church. You would be wise to get on her good side. You'll just have to change."

Staring into space, Daniel rehearsed this latest exchange with his senior pastor a couple more times before he sighed again, stood up, and began trying to figure out what to do with the books and papers.

"Why can't they accept me as I am?" he thought. "I'll clean up this place, but I've never been a neat freak and I never will be!"

How to Discourage Staff

Lack of support from a senior pastor is only one of the reasons staff people become discouraged and leave a local parish. There are many reasons why youth pastors and others have a reputation for staying a short period of time.

Marketplace Standards

Mary Jane Wilkie believes many churches fail to follow practices that are standard in most work environments in today's workplace.[2] Typical conditions in the secular marketplace include the following:

- Prospective employees undergo an interview process that avoids questions asking for personal information.
- Management provides employees with job descriptions and, after they are hired, orientation.
- Health insurance and other benefits are standard.
- In a workplace that has several employees, management provides a manual outlining policies and procedures that govern working relationships.
- The typical employee receives regular evaluations from supervisors. Employees have opportunities to identify areas of growth as well as a chance to voice frustrations.
- They expect fair wages and regular increases based on merit.
- Employees anticipate respect for their boundaries, believing each employee will answer directly to his or her supervisor, with no one else making decisions about an employee's duties and responsibilities.

Common Practice in the Local Church

These practices are often not the norm in local churches, according to Ms. Wilkie. Instead, common practices in many local churches may include the following:

- Supervisors expect employees to provide date of birth and marital status.
- Most churches do not participate in their state's unemployment or disability system, so laid-off employees receive no benefits in many states. The question for most churches is not whether they provide such benefits, but whether they inform employees before they hire them.
- A parishioner may bring a complaint against a church staff member and the senior pastor may use this information to dismiss a staff member with no further investigation or without trying to resolve the disharmony between parties. The case in the introduction to this chapter provides an example. Besides discouraging and demoralizing the staff member, such practices can leave the church open to a lawsuit.

> **The Best Place**
>
> A nine-word employment policy: "The best place for the best people to work."
>
> —Dale Dauten

- Churches often try to get by with the minimum in salary and benefits instead of building a strong relationship and solid loyalty among its staff persons.
- If a staff member makes a reasonable decision, but a parishioner complains, a senior pastor may override the decision, resulting in a disillusioned staff person, who is likely to leave.
- Many churches have buildings and grounds committees. Fewer have personnel committees. "Do we care more about buildings than people?" asks Ms. Wilkie.

Given these examples it's no wonder churches have a difficult time retaining quality staff persons.

The Insecure Boss

It's easy to blame lack of staff retention on either a disgruntled staff member or a senior pastor who does not manage well. Wayne Jacobsen believes neither is the case most of the time. "Staff members are just not that rebellious nor senior pastors that incompetent. Assigning blame at either point misses, in most cases, the real issue and only perpetuates conflict."[3]

Intolerance of a Subordinate's Success

Having said that, I point to King Saul as the exception—the boss who discourages employees. For one thing, he did not tolerate a subordinate's success. Following David's victory over Goliath, "Saul kept David with him and did not let him return to his father's house" (1 Sam. 18:2). When Saul sent David on any mission, David completed it successfully, with the result that Saul gave him a high rank in his army.

When the men returned from the campaign against the giant, the women from all the towns of Israel came out to meet King Saul and his army. Because of the great victory, they literally danced in the streets. Their celebration included singing, accompanied by tambourines and lutes. The women made up a song: "Saul has slain his thousands, and David his tens of thousands" (1 Sam. 18:7).

Saul fumed. With this kind of popularity, he reasoned, what more could David achieve than to wrestle the kingdom from the monarch's grasp?

Earlier, in pre-Goliath days, Saul had enlisted David's services as a harpist. The quiet music calmed the regent's troubled spirit. Now, with the galling refrain echoing in his ears, even David's harp-playing no longer soothed him. Twice Saul took a spear and hurled it at David, intending to pin the younger man to the wall. Young, agile David eluded the spear both times.

A senior pastor who hires a capable assistant runs the same risk as Saul did when he promoted David. Gregarious, competent staff pastors will develop friendships with laypersons who may have greater loyalty to the staff person than they have to the senior pastor. The latter must check his ego at the door and recognize that each person on his staff will be able to minister better to some people than the senior pastor can. And that's okay. In fact, it's a strength. Together, they minister to more people and do it more effectively than the senior pastor could do alone.

Likewise, the staff pastor must refuse to exploit these newly developed loyalties. Human nature being what it is, laypersons may complain about the senior pastor to the staff person. They may offer criticisms. The staff pastor must be determined to support his superior. If there are legitimate concerns he can share at an appropriate time with his supervising pastor, this is certainly appropriate. But if the staff pastor begins to cultivate criticism of his senior pastor, this behavior is wrong and will probably result in a parting of ways.

A wise senior pastor promotes his staff ministers, mentors them toward successful ministry, and rejoices in their achievements. Jealousy drives wedges that may never heal. A magnanimous spirit sets a better tone for all concerned.

Pitting One Subordinate Against Another

Saul is the antithesis of a good boss in another way: He tried to pit one subordinate against another.

One of the rewards for killing Goliath was the hand of the king's daughter in marriage. David refused, believing he was unworthy to be the king's son-in-law. Later, Michal, Saul's daughter, fell in love with David. Saul was pleased to know this because, he said, "I will give her to him, . . . so that she may be a snare to him and so that the hand of the Philistines may be against him" (1 Sam. 18:21).

Further, "Saul told his son Jonathan and all the attendants to kill David" (1 Sam. 19:1). Jonathan was too loyal to David to allow his father to use him in this way. But Saul's intent was to use Michal, Jonathan, or whomever he could enlist to get rid of David.

An insecure senior pastor may resort to such measures, encouraging competition between staff members, showing overt favoritism toward one staff person to the neglect of others, or even criticizing a staff member publicly, which is almost unforgiveable. What leaders fail to realize is that such behavior says more about their insecurity and poor leadership ability than it says about their staff.

Failing to Keep Your Word

Another weakness of Saul is that he didn't keep his word. David and his men were hiding in a cave when Saul entered, unaware that the young man was there. David slipped up behind him and cut off a corner of his robe. When Saul left the cave, David became conscience-stricken, went out of the cave, and spoke to the king. Bowing in humility before the monarch,

David wanted to know why the king pursued him.

When Saul understood David could have killed him in the cave, it unnerved the king. He admitted he had treated David badly. He acknowledged that David would one day be the king and asked David not to destroy Saul's descendants. In all this, Saul implied he would not harm David.

In subsequent days, Saul renewed his pursuit of the young man. Again, David crept up while Saul was asleep and took his spear and water jug.

The Best Policy

The pastor who on varying issues alternately placates a staff member by giving in and then denies something else to test commitment is not being honest. Neither is the staff member who attempts to manipulate the pastor by not providing all the facts about a decision or hides some pet project for fear the pastor will disapprove.

—Wayne Jacobsen

When he was a safe distance away, David called out to Saul, reminding him that for the second time he could have taken his life. Again Saul blessed David, but who could believe it came from a sincere heart?

Senior pastors who say one thing and do another are not only dishonest, they also cause frustration among their staff. Making promises and failing to follow through, far from building loyalty, breeds distrust and cynicism.

Building a Strong Staff

Some of the great churches of America have long-term staff members. Senior pastors like Bill Hybels of Willow Creek Community Church, Rick Warren of Saddleback Church, and many others hire good people who stay with them many years.

What are some things that build a strong staff that has staying power, thus strengthening a church for greater ministry?

Generous Compensation

David Lyons, president and CEO of MinisterSearch, says, "Construct a fair and competitive compensation plan based on their performances, including bonuses."[4] What's a fair and competitive compensation plan? Each year, Christianity Today and Church Law and Tax Report publish the *Compensation Handbook for Church Staff.* It "provides reliable church employee compensation breakdowns for part-time, full-time, church size, income budget, and geographical setting. With this information, you can compare your plan to other churches that have similar positions and demographics."[5]

Chapter 2 explores funding for staff expansion. Be sure you weigh the costs of hiring versus not hiring, as well as the costs for hiring well and hiring poorly.

As important as generous compensation is, money cannot do it all. "People working in non-profit organizations do not base their employment choices solely on financial compensation. More important than money is goodwill, the single factor most likely to keep employees loyal. Concern for an employee's well being, backed by actions that show the concern is genuine, will go a long way to offset a lower salary level."[6]

Clear Expectations

This involves a reasonable job description. I say "reasonable" because sometimes a church will overreact to a bad experience they had with a former staff member. They tend to put lots of details in the job description so they can send a clear signal that anyone who works here must be sure to do certain things and avoid others. Senior pastors can create opportunities to inform a new employee as to the church's particular culture, but to try to put every nuance in a job description can create an intimidating document.

A job description that paints with broad brush strokes the major things expected of a staff pastor is a much better approach. You will find helpful ideas about putting together a job description in chapter 4.

+≻— ≺+

A Pay Scale?

Often there are items in the budget that are less critical than taking care of your staff. What if they're at the top of your scale? Who says there has to be a scale? Gone are the days of a pecking order or levels of pay within an organization.

—David Lyons

Clear Lines of Communication

A friend of mine, a senior pastor whom I will call Roger, had lunch with his denominational supervisor. The supervisor had spoken with an assistant pastor named Dave on Roger's staff. In meeting with the supervisor, Dave had no particular gripe and was not trying to circumvent Roger's authority. The assistant was not well acquainted with the supervisor, and the purpose of their meeting was to get to know one another.

"Dave enjoys working with you," said the supervisor, when he and the senior pastor had lunch. "But he would like more communication. He would like to feel he knows your heart better."

Roger paid attention and invited Dave for breakfast on a weekly basis. They didn't always talk shop. Sometimes they talked about family. Other times they discussed church concerns. But the weekly breakfasts created a bond between the two that improved their working relationship. They still had staff meetings as usual that focused on church business, but it was the breakfast meetings that improved their communication.

In a survey, only 32 percent of staff pastors considered themselves well-informed about things they needed to know, yet twice that many—64 percent—declared such information was important to their satisfaction in the ministry.[7]

Strong Leadership

"In a well-run church, strong leadership provides vision, and helps staff feel they are part of something that matters."[8] The kind of leadership the senior pastor provides contributes a great deal to staff satisfaction. Willingness to develop the staff's leadership skills is an extension of good leadership. Providing books, seminars, funds for continuing education, and time for personal and professional development will help retain staff.

A wise senior pastor gets to know the strengths and weaknesses of his staff over time. With this knowledge, the supervisor can take advantage of strengths and encourage staff persons to shore up their weaknesses.

Effective Performance Reviews

Here are some suggestions for conducting positive performance reviews.

Make the process an annual, routine function. People are nervous about reviews. None of us really likes to be analyzed, scrutinized, or criticized. Yet by making it a routine part of the calendar, at least annually, it helps to avoid the appearance of calling a review just to deal with a specific problem. On the other hand, it gives the senior pastor the opportunity to deal with specific problems in the context of an overall review. This helps the supervisor to focus on the staff person's strengths and successes, which are usually in the majority, while not neglecting the areas where growth is needed.

Timing is important. Try to find a time in the calendar when the staff is not under a great deal of stress about other things. For instance, right before Easter or Christmas is not a good time for performance reviews. Right after these events may also be poor times because people may be exhausted. As difficult as it may be, try to find a time when the schedule eases a little.

Give the staff person the opportunity to review him- or herself. If your review includes a form on which the staff person checks a number of qualities on a scale of one to five, you can compare the way they rate themselves with the way you see them. It also gives them a chance to talk about the areas in which they would like to see improvement.

Change evaluation tools from time to time. If we do the same thing the same way every time, it becomes too much a part of the routine. The tendency is not to be completely candid. It's not that the staff person is trying to deceive or be dishonest. A familiar test can elicit expected answers rather than ones that are thought through.

Use the tool to affirm. Even though you may have to address weaknesses or mistakes, the conscientious staff member has more positive qualities than negative, more successes than failures. If he or she has made too many mistakes and is not working up to par, especially if a dismissal is the only viable option, no evaluation tool can cover the errors. You will still have to be firm and perhaps initiate a termination.

Retaining Good People

I don't know any senior pastors who enjoy hiring and firing. They would much rather find good people and keep them as long as possible. What are some keys to retaining effective staff people?

Build Goodwill

Creating an atmosphere of collegiality and congeniality seldom happens by accident. As Norman Shawchuck says, "Senior ministers should pay close attention to the care, feeding and motivation of staff."[9]

Creating a sense of camaraderie on a church staff may be as simple as praying together on a regular basis for the church prayer requests. Getting together socially can be valuable. Jacobsen cites such key terms as *respect, understanding, freedom, submission, deference, honesty,* and *openness* as important in disarming conflict and encouraging warm relationships.[10]

Developing personal friendships will contribute toward a spirit of goodwill on the staff. So will supporting one another. Jesus told his disciples, "You are my friends" (John 15:14). Should a church staff say less?

Having close relationships on a church staff does not mean we always agree. Good friends know they can

Accountability

All persons should be held accountable for standards, goals, and actions, and managers do no kindness by nurturing dysfunction. In fact, employees do not respect a manager who tolerates slipshod performance (and they know the difference). Expecting employees to give their best is one of the traits of a good leader.

—Mary Jane Wilkie

disagree without being disagreeable. Jesus loved Peter but he also rebuked him (Mark 8:33).

Encourage Creativity and Responsibility

Blessed is the pastor who gives a staff person an assignment and gets out of the way. Perhaps a pastor is thinking, "I'm not sure I can trust the staff person with that much freedom." If that's the case, perhaps you need to hire better people. Or perhaps you need to learn how to let go and trust your staff.

Subordinates become frustrated when a supervisor gives an assignment and then micromanages how they do their work. There's usually no one right way to do anything. God has put infinite creativity into our working processes. Giving people latitude tells them you trust them. If they don't perform to your satisfaction, you can make it a teachable opportunity and both of you learn better how to work together.

Staff members love it when a senior pastor recognizes them as professionals in their own right, ministers who are capable of carrying out their own area of ministry. Nobody likes to think he or she is a "go-fer," but they do appreciate being treated as colleagues.

Professor and author George Odiorne describes supervisors who manage people in ways that cause their staff to shrink rather than grow. He calls them "people shrinkers."[11] People tend to shrink when managers do not give them significant areas of responsibility and allow them to either succeed or fail.

Don't Move the Target Too Often

Staff members become frustrated when the focus changes too often. When the supervisor makes a sudden shift in direction and then does it again with a short period of time, subordinates may become irritated.

Working together on specific goals can unite a staff. Moving the target can bring disunity. Altering goals suddenly, without warning, generates confusion and dissatisfaction.

If the senior pastor decides to change direction, he is wise to bring the staff together, discuss the issues, ask for input, and build consensus rather than announcing an arbitrary shift.

Give Support

A church that adds its first staff member may well hire a younger person, perhaps someone fresh out of college or seminary. An inexperienced person looks to the senior pastor for help. Even more experienced individuals appreciate a senior pastor's concern and helpful input.

A survey indicated 88 percent of staff members considered support very important, but only 57 percent felt they were receiving adequate support.

Hiring Decisions

Hiring decisions are tough. Bad hiring decisions are brutal.

—Jack Connell

One way a senior pastor can fail to give support is through inadequate communication. When a staff person seldom sees the senior minister outside the pulpit, seldom has a meaningful one-on-one conversation, and seldom senses any level of support, that staff person will become restless and begin looking for other opportunities. Don't let that happen. Show you care by offering and giving genuine support.

One associate summed up the senior pastor's support in a succinct comment: "He loves me, encourages me, corrects me, and shares his heart with me."[12]

Give Recognition

When senior pastors give sincere compliments to their staff, especially in public, it communicates more than gratitude. It tells the staff members, in huge letters, that they are appreciated, valued, and supported.

From the staff members' viewpoint, they feel like colleagues, not subordinates. Although they may provide genuine assistance, they don't feel like "assistants" when the senior minister provides deserved recognition.

Another way to provide recognition is to share some of the duties that are most rewarding. If the associate preaches, let him or her preach on occasion. If laypersons with whom they work closely are ready for baptism, why not let associates participate in the ritual. Serving the sacrament of the Lord's Supper is another way to include staff persons who not only enjoy the experience, but feel acknowledged as colleagues who are qualified and capable.

Supporting Staff

Mrs. Gibson continued her complaints about Daniel, the youth pastor, until he felt the best thing was to resign and find employment elsewhere. Regrettably, his senior pastor did nothing to help him and did not encourage him to stay. It was easier to let him go than to confront Mrs. Gibson with her misplaced criticisms.

Jimmy Johnson, a long-term youth pastor at Skyline Wesleyan Church in San Diego, used to tell about a woman who kept pressing him to shape up her son who was in Jimmy's high school youth group. In frustration, Jimmy told her that her son was a good kid and she ought to get off the boy's back. While the woman stood there, mouth gaping at Jimmy's brashness, he turned and strode away.

After the mother approached Dr. Orval Butcher, founding pastor of Skyline, he called Jimmy into his office. Dr. Butcher had told the mother, "Jimmy knows those kids and he loves them." In his firm, quiet demeanor, he added, "If he says you ought to get off your son's back, you probably ought to get off his back."

In a private conversation with Jimmy, Dr. Butcher said, "Now, Jimmy, what you said was correct, but you must find a different way to express yourself."

Dr. Butcher retained a valuable staff member, while both supporting and correcting him.

Action Steps

1. Think about how you can show support and recognition to your current staff members.
2. Consider the level of creativity and responsibility you are giving current staff. How could you improve it?
3. Assess the level of camaraderie on your staff. How strong are the friendships? How is the staff showing support for one another? What can you do to improve it?

7

MANAGEMENT
Becoming a Terrific Boss

*A senior pastor can become a terrific boss both
by what he stops doing and by what he starts doing.*

I read about a young man working on a graduate degree who spent a summer with one of the Native American tribes in the southwestern United States. As a project for his curriculum, he immersed himself in their culture, ate their food, learned their customs, and participated in every way he could with their daily lives.

He communicated with them as best he could, even learning some of their language. Over the months of his residency among them, he became close to some of them. He saw them, not as objects for examination and research, but as people with unique cultural challenges.

> The best executive is the one who has sense enough to pick good men to do what he wants done, and self-restraint enough to keep from meddling with them while they do it.
>
> —Theodore Roosevelt[1]

He became particularly close to an older woman, who was a matriarch among her people. When the time came for him to leave, he especially regretted having to tell her goodbye.

Standing before her, trying to express his appreciation for her help and friendship, he struggled for just the right words to say. She sensed his difficulty and drew near to him. Taking his face in both her hands, she said, "I like me best when I'm with you."

Imagine my surprise when I read the words of Peter Schutz, the former CEO of Porsche, who described a working relationship with a colleague: "I like *me* best when I'm around *you*."[2]

I wonder how many employees would say that about their bosses. My guess: not many. Most bosses have the default role of supervisor. Supervision seldom comes with warm fuzzy feelings connected to it. We tend to associate supervision with concepts like accountability, reporting, and having someone look over our shoulders. An elementary school principal once explained to a first-grade teacher what he was doing outside her door, peering through the glass, observing her teaching. "I'm snoopervising," he said, without apology.

To become terrific bosses, we'll definitely have to get beyond "snoopervising."

Excellence Prevention

What attitudes and behaviors keep senior pastors from becoming terrific bosses? What ruts can they fall into, condemning them to a negative image, as far as staff is concerned?

A Dictatorial Attitude

Dictatorships produce efficient governments because they bring violence and discord under control. They produce a quiet and predictable lifestyle. They also squash creativity. They dis-

courage thinking outside the box. Top-down leadership can produce a chain reaction. The boss growls at an employee, the
employee goes home and snaps at his wife. The wife snarls at the
children, who kick the dog, who chases the neighborhood cat.[3]

It's easy to fall into this trap, even in church work, if we forget who our model is. Jesus exemplified servant leadership. If
they're not careful, senior pastors can adopt a superior attitude.
The staff exists to carry out their wishes, they seem to think.
There is a degree of truth to this, of course. The senior pastor
casts the vision and leads the way. But being a servant-leader is
a Christlike model, in which the senior must lead, not drive. He
must lift, not dominate.

Being Too Task-Oriented

Most leaders, it seems, are task-oriented, by definition. It's
their job to get things done. The problem is people keep getting
in the way.

Henri Nouwen remembered an old professor at Notre Dame.
Reflecting on a long life of teaching, the professor said, "I have
always been complaining that my work was constantly interrupted,
until I slowly discovered that my interruptions were my work."

Nouwen observed, "This is the great conversion in life: to
recognize and believe that the many unexpected events are not
just disturbing interruptions of our projects, but the way in
which God molds our hearts and prepares us for his return. . . ."[4]

While many tasks are crucial, and we pay people to get
things done, we must remember that the people are more important than the tasks. A pastor friend told me that when he was the
new senior minister at a church, one of his leading laymen, a

successful businessman, said, "What we need is somebody who will call on the customers."

Long ago doctors made house calls. So did pastors. In many places, the laypersons do not want pastoral visits because their lives are already crowded. Even if routine "calling on the customers" is no longer our practice, we must find a way to place a higher value on people, both staff and laypersons.

Delegating Poorly

Poor delegation results in frustrated staff members. Pastors delegate poorly when they aren't specific enough. Or when they delegate the task, and then look over the staff person's shoulder, "snoopervising." Or when they delegate the matter, but take it back again because it isn't being done well enough, fast enough, or up to the senior pastor's standards.

Abraham Lincoln knew how to delegate and empower others. He told Ulysses S. Grant, when he appointed him as commander of the Union armies in 1864, "I neither ask nor desire to know anything of your plans. Take the responsibility and act, and call on me for assistance."[5]

Staff members may also become frustrated when their supervising pastor delegates a job and gives too many details on exactly how the job must be done. Almost every job can be done in a variety of ways, most of them

---

Why Leaders Don't Delegate

- Fear of losing authority
- Fear of work being done poorly
- Fear of work being done *better*
- Unwillingness to take the necessary time
- Fear of depending on others
- Lack of training and positive experience

—Hans Finzel

equally effective. Insisting it be done a certain way stifles creativity and leaves the staff member feeling he or she is not trusted.

Insincerity

People know whether you really care about them or not. Staff members quickly discern whether your concern is genuine or if it's just talk. The late megachurch pastor Jerry Falwell said, "My goal is to let [people] know they are important to me and to God. To make a person aware that he or she is of great importance to you, you must show genuine interest."

He went on to say, "They won't share if you don't care. As quickly as possible, make people know that you care about their accomplishments and their burdens, . . . and it's got to be genuine."[6]

Biblical Guidelines for Being a Terrific Boss

Paul wrote to Timothy about the qualifications of overseers and deacons (1 Tim. 3:1–13). Later in the letter to his protégé, he offered guidelines on how to treat those who are in the ministry (5:17–22). In this passage John Stott sees five principles for dealing with those under our care.[7] They provide helpful guidelines for a senior pastor who wants to be a terrific boss to his staff.

Appreciation

"The elders who direct the affairs of the church well are worthy of double honor, especially those whose work is preaching and teaching. For the Scripture says, 'Do not muzzle the ox while

117

it is treading out the grain,' and 'The worker deserves his wages'" (1 Tim. 5:17–18).

By citing two other passages of Scripture, the first from Deuteronomy 25:4 and the second from Luke 10:7, Paul reinforces his idea that workers in the church should be well paid. The concept of "double honor" may not necessarily refer to twice the pay of others (he does not specify which others). Rather, it may mean the double honor of both financial payment and respect.

Showing appreciation by affirming others and their work is the very least we can do, along with as generous a salary as possible. Nobody is immune from the need for appreciation. Abraham Lincoln, considered by many as our greatest president, valued words of affirmation. A display in the Smithsonian Institution verifies this. It contains the personal effects found on the body of Lincoln the night of his assassination: a small handkerchief embroidered "A. Lincoln," a country boy's penknife, a spectacle case repaired with cotton string, a Confederate five-dollar bill, and a worn-out newspaper clipping extolling his accomplishments as president. It begins, "Abe Lincoln is one of the greatest statesmen of all time. . . ."[8]

Lincoln faced fierce criticism while he was in office. Undoubtedly that article helped him keep his mission in perspective. In a similar way, a senior minister's words of appreciation can boost a staff member's flagging confidence.

Fairness

"Do not entertain an accusation against an elder unless it is brought by two or three witnesses. Those who sin are

to be rebuked publicly, so that the others may take warning"
(1 Tim. 5:19–20).

Senior pastors need great wisdom because eventually someone
will criticize a staff member. John Calvin said, "None are more
exposed to slanders and insults than godly teachers." Even
when Christian workers perform their duties conscientiously
and well, they "never avoid a thousand criticisms."[9]

When accusations come, the senior pastor must be sure they
are not gossip. The charges must be substantiated by several
persons. If Pastor Sam, in the previous chapter, had paid attention
to this Scripture passage, he would have handled both his youth
pastor and Mrs. Gibson differently.

On the other side of the coin, when the charges are true, the
pastor must be careful how he responds. A rule of thumb is that
he should deal with private sins privately and public sins publicly. Nobody wants to deal with charges of wrongdoing, but it's
part of the job, and only a wise and fair senior pastor, led by the
Spirit, will handle it well.

Impartiality

"I charge you, in the sight of God and Christ Jesus and the
elect angels, to keep these instructions without partiality, and to
do nothing out of favoritism" (1 Tim. 5:21).

The children in a Catholic elementary school lined up for lunch.
As they moved through the line, they saw a note by the apples,
placed there by a nun: "Take only ONE . . . God is watching."

Further down the line, by a large plate of chocolate chip
cookies, a child had placed a note: "Take all you want. God is
watching the apples."

Equal Treatment

There is nothing so
unequal as the equal
treatment of unequals.

—Kenneth Blanchard

In truth, God can watch the apples and the cookies, as well as our behavior, all at the same time. So it places a great burden of responsibility on the leader to deal with staff without partiality.

As humans, we have our favorites. We click better with some people than with others. Further, being impartial does not mean equal treatment, even as a wise parent knows the same kind of discipline will not work equally with all the children.

Yet, to the best of our ability, we must reject favoritism and apply impartiality in all our dealings.

Caution

"Do not be hasty in the laying on of hands, and do not share in the sins of others. Keep yourself pure. Stop drinking only water, and use a little wine because of your stomach and your frequent illnesses" (1 Tim. 5:22–23).

Senior pastors may or may not be directly involved in the "laying on of hands" of staff persons, especially if a staff member is ordained by a denominational authority. A pastor may "lay on hands" in a commissioning or installation process when a new person joins the staff.

In either case, as Bob Black says, "Ordination councils have a tough job, but they owe it to the church and to the candidates who come before them to ask tough questions and make tough choices. To be careless in the selection of Christian leaders is to 'share in the sins of others' when those improperly or negligently ordained elders fall."[10]

Discernment

"The sins of some men are obvious, reaching the place of judgment ahead of them; the sins of others trail behind them. In the same way, good deeds are obvious, and even those that are not cannot be hidden" (1 Tim. 5:24–25).

To be terrific bosses, we must learn to hire well. This requires discernment. Often people who seem dynamic and well suited for ministry have hidden flaws and weaknesses. Others who appear reticent and unassuming may have strengths that are not immediately apparent. Stott calls it the "iceberg principle, namely that nine-tenths of a person are hidden from view."[11]

So the senior pastor must take the time to get acquainted with the candidate, using the resume, interview, references, and testing, as outlined in Chapter 5. While no perfect candidates exist, senior ministers need to be aware of both strengths and weaknesses. This knowledge enables the supervisor to utilize the gifts and strengths of his staff to best advantage while minimizing the impact of weaknesses.

Leadership Styles for Managing Staff

I mentioned earlier that just as no two children should be treated alike, staff members respond to different kinds of leadership. Don Cousins observed, "Some people need a tight leash, others space. Some need to be shown clearly, almost harshly, when they blunder, because their characteristic response to mistakes is a blasé, 'Oh well.' Others need only a gentle prod, because they've already died a thousand deaths over their error."[12]

Knowing what kind of leadership to use with each staff person requires wisdom. Ken Blanchard cites four types of leadership styles, which he calls "situational leadership."[13] Which one a leader uses depends on the worker's competence and confidence.

Direction

When new staff members lack experience, they need direction. Either because they're fresh out of college or seminary, or because they're beginning to work in a new field, they need more hands-on guidance than a person with experience. Even if they have experience, but are new to your church, they must learn your systems, your church's culture, and a new set of expectations.

We have all needed direction at one point or another in life. As Yogi Berra said, in his inimitable way, "If you don't know where you're going, you may end up someplace else."

Doug Firebaugh says it's easy to lose your way because we forget that we need a "lantern of reality" and a "compass of flexibility." The senior minister can provide the "lantern of reality" by putting the subordinate's role in context. "Here's what this job looks like in this situation, with these people, in this location." The pastor can also extend a "compass of flexibility" by letting the staffer know that missing the mark occasionally is possible and permissible, as long as it's not continually repeated.

Coaching

Some staff people have experience and skill, but still need a degree of direction. These individuals need coaching.

Often we think of coaching in terms of athletic teams, as a basketball or football coach. Another way to look at coaching is to see it as a variation of the word *coach*. Before a coach was a person who directed an athletic team, a coach was a vehicle for transporting people from one location to another.

To coach staff people, the senior pastor first needs to discuss with them where they want to go. Once they have a clear direction, which may include direct input from the supervisor, they can talk about how to get there. The senior pastor, or coach, then supports the staffers in their efforts to accomplish the goals.

Denominational executive Thomas Armiger cites three ingredients for a good coaching relationship.

Availability. It takes time to develop people, but that's the commitment a senior pastor must make, for the sake of the kingdom, before he hires staff. The payoff is seeing that staff member grow into a stronger, more effective leader.

Accountability. A relationship involving accountability must be built around honesty and truth telling. Paul is our example. He taught the value of "speaking the truth in love" as an essential ingredient to help us "grow up into him who is the Head, that is, Christ" (Eph. 4:15).

Ability. A coach must be willing to transfer skills to the person being coached. This is especially valuable for an inexperienced staffer or one who is entering a new field of endeavor. We have all picked up skills from others who coached us. This is "paying it forward" by investing in the lives of others.[14]

Support

This style of leadership recognizes that staff people have the skills needed to do the job. Thus they require little direct input as to *how* a task should be accomplished. They do, however, need support from the senior pastor. Often that support will come in the form of praise and encouragement.

As I've said elsewhere, "Top performers don't work for money alone. They're also motivated by an internal desire to achieve. Workers who are concerned with excellence have an inner source of inspiration. Good leaders recognize these excellence seekers when they see them and tap their hidden resources by praising their achievements."

Create an atmosphere of affirmation and you will succeed. When we bend over backward to support and encourage good workers, our praise acts as a stimulant to spur them on to even greater accomplishments. If you want to be a terrific boss, be supportive by praising sincerely and often.

> **The Power of Encouragement**
>
> I have never seen a man who could do real work except under the stimulus of encouragement and enthusiasm, and the approval of the people for whom he is working.
>
> —Charles Schwab

Delegation

To a more seasoned staff person a senior pastor can delegate assignments completely. The subordinate has responsibility for making decisions, solving the problems, and getting the job done.

As Lorne Sanny observes, every subordinate asks four questions:

- What am I supposed to do?
- Will you let me do it?
- Will you help me when I need it?
- Will you let me know how I'm doing?[15]

Delegating doesn't mean the senior pastor ignores his staffer. It does mean that once delegated, he or she must not take the matter back unless the staff person asks for assistance. One of the keys to making this system work is to communicate well in the first place. Putting the assignment in writing is not a bad policy.

You can build up a subordinate's confidence by assigning low-risk projects until they gain experience. Assigning a due date is also advisable. If you haven't talked with your employee for awhile, it's appropriate to check with him or her as the deadline draws closer.

As I indicated earlier in this chapter, be sure you let the staff person do the project his or her way. It may even be better than the way you would have done it. If you made the right decision in hiring them, they probably have some great ideas.

Blessed is the senior pastor who understands he cannot lead all staff members in the same way. As we learn how to deal with individuals according to their competence and confidence, we have the joy of witnessing their movement from needing direction to coaching to support to being able to delegate matters to them in full confidence that they will handle them well.

Becoming a Terrific Boss

Every supervisor would like to be a terrific boss. But such a reputation isn't based on your ambition. It's based on how well you supervise others and how they view your leadership. In addition to the other recommendations in this chapter, consider these positive and practical ideas for excelling as a supervising pastor.

Communicate Well

The first rule of communication is to listen. How will you know what is going on in your church if you are not listening to your staff, to your board, and to your laypeople? Do constituents and staff really understand your vision? Are rumors flying around that have only a grain of truth but great amounts of misinformation? You'll find out if you listen.

Jesse Ventura, the former governor of Minnesota, said, "When I ran for governor, nobody thought I could win. But I never tried to hide who I am, in conversations, speeches, whatever, and people came out and voted in record numbers. But I also think listening is as important as talking. It's interesting: If you're a good listener, people often compliment you for being a good conversationalist."[16]

In another context I've talked about the importance of communication: "People may forget what you say, but they'll never forget how you say it. Be positive. Lift others up, and they'll follow you."

Clarify Your Vision

A sage once advised, "Stay one step ahead of your people and you are called a leader. Stay ten steps ahead of your people and you are called a martyr!"

Most of us don't have the problem of being too far out in front. Some senior pastors do suffer from a case of fuzzy vision. Because they're not clear about where they want to go, their uncertainty trickles down to the staff. It can manifest itself as a malaise and a sense of dissatisfaction. Then a cloud of melancholy can settle over their subordinates.

When vision is fuzzy, workers lose interest. People who work on assembly lines, putting the same bolt in the same slot month after month often stay motivated because they get paid very well. Most church staffers do not get paid high salaries. So their motivation must be linked to a dream, a vision, a direction.

Hans Finzel tells about a square marble stone with a brass marker perched prominently in the front yard of a suburban house in Wheaton, Illinois. In the midst of his jog, he stopped to read it, expecting to find something historically significant. It read: *On This Spot in 1897 Nothing Happened.* He felt foolish and wondered if anyone had been watching from a window, just to see his reaction.[17]

How sad if someone placed on the church lawn a marker that said: "Due to lack of vision, nothing happened here." On the other hand, a simple plaque could never tell the story of what happens when the senior pastor leads with vision and the staff members get on board, each contributing his or her expertise.

Hiring Decisions

All men dream, but not equally.

Those who dream by night in the dusty recesses of their minds

Awake to find that it was vanity;

But the dreams of day are dangerous men,

That they may act their dreams with open eyes to make it possible.

—T. E. Lawrence

David Rockefeller has been quoted as saying, "The number one function of the top executive is to establish the purpose of the organization."[18]

Learn to Appreciate Mavericks

In the 2008 presidential campaign, Arizona Senator John McCain and Alaska Governor Sarah Palin described themselves as mavericks who would "clean up" Washington and bring about needed change. Their efforts were not quite enough to win the White House, but they certainly brought the idea of mavericks into the limelight.

The mavericks you want to encourage are creative people who think outside the box, but do it in a way that is consistent with your vision and goals. Youth pastors are famous (or infamous) for being mavericks. They want to reach the younger generation who frequently don't respond to the same things that appeal to their parents and grandparents. You may cringe at the techniques and off-the-wall antics of youth pastors, but as long as they get the job done, are respectful of others who aren't on their wave length, and achieve the church's mission, we ought to give them some slack.

Mavericks you don't want to encourage are those who have their own agenda, care very little about the church's history, culture, and structure, and are truly rebellious. If they won't listen to your counsel, don't respect your authority, and are disdainful of those who disagree with them, you're probably better off if they move on to another assignment.

If they're making a difference, if others are following their leadership, and if they're producing good results consistent with your vision, encourage them any way you can. True, they may need a long leash. Eagles can't soar if they're tied down. Believe in them, encourage them, rein them in when you must. But do it in such a way that they learn, profit from the experience, and continue to grow.

Understand that, by definition, mavericks do not work well with committees, tedious policy manuals, indecision, or "snoopervision."

Just remember, to the religious establishment of his day, Jesus was a maverick. To the Pharisees, so was Paul. And so was Stephen. Mavericks have a reputation as being trouble-makers, but the fact is, they are wired differently than others. They are willing to take more risks than most people. And they need a lot of flexibility.

Flexibility

A statesman gains little by the arbitrary exercise of ironclad authority upon all occasions that offer, for this wounds the just pride of his subordinates, and thus tends to undermine his strength. The little concession, now and then, where it can do no harm is the wise policy.

—Mark Twain

If you can learn to appreciate them and work with them, they can accomplish great things for the kingdom of God, help you in achieving your vision, and help establish your reputation as a terrific boss.

A Hard-Earned Reputation

Gordon MacDonald tells about a person who applied for a job and presented recommendations from a pastor and a Sunday school teacher. After studying the complimentary things these people said, the manager told the young person, "I'm impressed with the nice things these people have said about you. It's obvious that you appear to them to be just what we need. But I would very much like a recommendation from someone who is acquainted with your activities on the weekdays."[19]

The people who will determine whether you are a terrific boss are not those who listen to you only on Sunday. They are the staff members who see your leadership through the week.

A friend confided that he felt special warmth when a subordinate in the ministry said, "You are the best supervisor I've ever had. I've learned so much from you."

Such a reputation does not come easily. It comes from hard work, genuine concern for people, and a willingness to invest in the lives of others.

Mark Twain said, "Let us endeavor so to live that when we come to die even the undertaker will be sorry."

The evaluation that really counts is the final one given by the Lord himself. "When it comes time to present your work to the One who called you, you want to be able to present Him with exactly what He asked for."[20]

Action Steps

1. Think about the balance in your life between being task-oriented and people-oriented. How does this affect your treatment of staff? What changes do you need to make?
2. If you have staff, even volunteer workers, which ones need direction? Which ones need coaching? Support? Delegation?
3. How often have you emphasized your vision for the church in the past six months? How will you clarify your vision for staff and congregation? When?

8

STRATEGY
Building for Growth and Expansion

*The church is not ready to add staff until the pastor
spends the necessary time in restructuring the
church for growth and expansion.*

Pastor Duane listened to the last strains of the organ, where his wife Sandra sat, as he focused intently on the closing measures of the prelude. As soon as the last chord reverberated in the sanctuary, he strode to the pulpit and led the congregation in the invocation.

He asked them to take their hymnals and turn to the opening song, which he proceeded to direct. Others might use video projectors, but his church preferred the hymnal and that suited him just fine. After a couple of songs and a responsive reading, he announced the offering, whereupon two aged ushers ambled forward to retrieve the plates.

> A church with a solo pastor will stop growing when it reaches the limit of the pastor's ability to successfully handle all of the priorities.
>
> —Gary L. McIntosh

While Pastor Duane led in the offertory prayer, Sandra slipped quietly behind him from the organ to the piano. After her husband said, "Amen," she began an inspirational offertory on the piano. She finished with a flourish and hurried back to the organ while her husband announced the prayer chorus.

As he prayed the pastoral prayer, she shuttled back to the piano. After the prayer, she accompanied herself on a special song to set the mood for his message.

Every Sunday for years, it was the same. Except for the actual collection of the offering, Pastor Duane or Sandra did everything in the service.

When they retired, the church's reaction was mixed. Some despaired. "What will we do?" they said. "All these years, Pastor and his wife have done everything. Who will lead worship now?"

Others rejoiced. "All these years, Pastor and his wife have done everything. Finally, other capable people in the congregation will have opportunity to use their gifts."

Who Is Going to Do All the Work?

Pastor Duane and Sandra fell into the snare that Fred Smith described as a "Mom and Pop" operation.[1] Like some small businesses, a pastor and his wife will run the church. In a small business, Pop runs the counter, while Mom counts the money in the back room. Or if Pop is better at handling money and Mom is better at handling customers, they switch roles.

Either way, sooner or later, Mom and Pop feel tired and harassed. The store can't function unless one of them is there. Every time the door opens, either Mom or Pop stands behind the counter. Their operation will never grow beyond a certain level because they have not discovered the secret of training and involving others in "running the store."

Some church members like this system, just like some customers like the familiar, comfortable feeling they have when they visit the corner grocery, or delicatessen, or whatever enterprise Mom and Pop are running. Others don't care for it and prefer to go to larger stores (churches) where the proprietors offer greater variety and more services.

In local churches run by Moms and Pops, the people who enjoy it remain loyal, because they don't have to make a huge commitment, beyond attending and contributing their money. Why should they get involved? Mom and Pop have it covered. Those who don't like it either drift away to other churches or stay and develop resentment.

The Mom and Pop operation meets the needs of a few who are comfortable with the Pastor Duanes and Sandras of the world running the show. However, the church bumps up against a glass ceiling that it can't penetrate as long as its vision is limited to what Mom and Pop can do.

Realigning the church toward a focus on growth and expansion becomes a high priority for any pastor who wants the church to be healthy. A healthy church is not one that is content to let a few people do everything. A healthy church is not one that is satisfied to see the same faces in worship week after week. A healthy church is not one that can go for years without seeing new believers coming to faith in Jesus Christ. A healthy church is not one that cares little for discipleship and allows people to flounder due to lack of spiritual formation.

But who is going to do all those things? Who is going to reach the lost? Who will disciple the new believers?

The first step toward answering these questions and developing a healthy church is not hiring staff. An earlier step must involve developing better lay leadership. Even when the church does hire staff, if a pastor has not developed lay leadership, the congregation will still depend on the staff to do all the things Mom and Pop used to do.

How many churches across North America see multitudes of laypeople coming and going every weekend, underutilized because no one challenges them to use their gifts and talents for God and the church?

If a pastor has not been successful in developing and managing a faithful corps of laypeople who are committed to minister according to their gifts, how will he manage additional paid staff?

Gifted to Work in the Church

When Moses felt overwhelmed with all the challenges of leading thousands of people across the wilderness toward the Promised Land, his first response was not to hire professional counselors or caseworkers. At the suggestion of his father-in-law, Jethro, he chose individuals to help him judge the people.

After affirming Moses' role as leader and teacher of the multitudes, Jethro advised,

But select capable men from all the people—men who fear God, trustworthy men who hate dishonest gain— and appoint them as officials over thousands, hundreds, fifties and tens. Have them serve as judges for the people at all times, but have them bring every difficult case to you; the simple cases they can decide themselves. That will make your load lighter, because they will share it with you. If you do this and God so commands, you will be able to stand the strain, and all these people will go home satisfied (Ex. 18:21–23).

Doing Ministry or Supervising Ministry?

It's the classic case of moving from doing ministry to seeing that ministry is done. This is a major step in growing a church. The pastor can't do it all himself. Mom and Pop together are better and stronger than either individual would be, but even their teamwork is limited. God has given people gifts to enable them to do the work of the ministry and to multiply the ministry of a few.

The apostle Paul wrote, "He [Christ] handed out gifts of apostle, prophet, evangelist, and pastor-teacher to train Christians in skilled servant work" (Eph. 4:11–12 MSG). Far from doing it all ourselves, God wants pastors to train others to do the work of the ministry. As I have said before, "Jesus modeled that for us. He combined ministry with training. The disciples learned to love and respect the Master as He poured His life into them. One-to-one or in small groups, the disciples learned the spiritual ropes."[2]

The Benefits of Using Spiritual Gifts

Consider the benefits. When we follow God's plan, Christians will be "working within Christ's body, the church, until we're all moving rhythmically and easily with each other, efficient and graceful in response to God's Son, fully mature adults, fully developed within and without, fully alive like Christ" (Eph. 4:12–13 MSG).

The payoff in maturity is colossal. This is how the church becomes healthy and stable. Paul continues:

> Then we will no longer be infants, tossed back and forth by the waves, and blown here and there by every wind of teaching and by the cunning and craftiness of men in their deceitful scheming. Instead, speaking the truth in love, we will in all things grow up into him who is the Head, that is, Christ. From him the whole body, joined and held together by every supporting ligament, grows and builds itself up in love, as each part does its work (Eph. 4:14–16).

In commenting on this passage, Maxie Dunnam says the metaphor Paul uses "is that of a boat bobbing up and down, veering here and there, controlled and tossed about by changing and erratic wind. Young children tend to believe everything they are told, and rudderless boats, or boats without someone at the helm, tend to go wherever the wind takes them. Christians are to be more mature, wiser, and more perceptive in order to recognize and withstand the cunning craftiness of those who would deceive."[3]

Maturity of the Members

Wouldn't it be different to hear a preacher say, "I want a church whose size will be determined by the maturity of the individual members"?

—Fred Smith, Sr.

With training and discipleship, our Christian workers will move beyond the childhood stage and will become mature workers. As both gifted and trained, they become healthy, solid bricks in the mortar of the church.

So pastors who want a healthy church must develop a strong cadre of Christian workers from among their laypersons. When the work becomes too demanding or too time-consuming for the laypeople, or the work requires greater expertise than the laypeople possess, the pastor must then begin to plan for adding staff.

A Strategy for Hiring Staff

When we are ready to hire staff, whom should we hire first? What guidelines should we use to determine a hiring strategy that will result in church growth?

Reaching and Keeping New People

As a pastor begins to see growth occur in his local church, it happens because either he or others in the congregation have found new people. Either church members have reached out to their friends, associates, neighbors, and relatives, or a new program emphasis has attracted visitors to the congregation.

We always have to ask four questions in church work:

1. How do we get people to come?
2. How do we get them to come back?
3. How do we get them to stay?
4. How do we get them involved?

The reason we ask these questions is because we not only want to reach people, we want to keep them. Besides reaching people and keeping them, we also celebrate with people. We worship with them. The early stages of any church include those three elements: reaching, keeping, and worshiping.

Maturing People

As time goes on, things become more complicated. We need to educate people or disciple them. Their spiritual formation becomes a prime concern because we don't want our people to remain spiritual infants. We want them to grow in grace.

As we begin to develop ministries that address spiritual formation, we soon find the organization is becoming complex enough that it now requires oversight. Youth ministries, children's ministries, small groups, perhaps women's and men's ministries have blossomed. Who is going to oversee all these ministries?

> **Investment**
>
> An organization ought to invest in that part of the organization that will immediately affect the community it seeks to reach.
>
> —Arthur DeKruyter

Further, the larger the church grows, the more needs we must address, so we develop a focus on caring for people. Weddings, funerals, hospital visitation, and counseling concerns all begin to crowd into a busy pastor's schedule.

Gary McIntosh cites six areas of priority and how we address them as crucial in determining whether a church will continue to grow or plateau. If we place great priority on reaching, keeping, and celebrating (worshiping), the church will grow. If the priority shifts to educating (discipling), overseeing, and caring for people, the church will enter a maintenance mode and will likely plateau.[4]

Which Staff Positions Will Help Us Grow?

Then we must ask ourselves, what kind of impact does hiring staff have on answering the four questions above? And what kind of impact does hiring staff have on dealing with the six areas of priority?

The trend in many churches is to fill the staff position that is most in vogue at the time. Years ago, the first person hired was the youth pastor. If the church couldn't afford a full-time youth pastor, the job might be a combination of responsibilities, such as youth and music, or youth and Christian education. We used to hire ministers of music. Now we hire worship arts pastors.

The real question is, what staff person will enable us to keep growing? The answer, it depends. It depends on the church's needs and on the gifts of the senior pastor.

If the senior pastor is gifted in reaching and keeping new people, the church would profit by hiring someone who can relieve him of some responsibilities in the discipleship, oversight, or caring areas. If the senior pastor has great administrative gifts and excels at oversight and caring for people, it would make sense to hire someone gifted in reaching and keeping people.

The Limit

One of the most difficult things a pastor has to do is gather a staff that can complement her or his gifts.

—Bill Easum

The boxer Rocky Balboa in the movie *Rocky* talks about how much he values the teamwork he feels with his girlfriend Adrian: "I've got gaps, she's got gaps. Together, we've got no gaps."[5]

The ideal in church staffing is to close the gaps so the senior pastor can excel in what he does best and others fill the areas that still need attention.

If the church has competent musicians who lead worship with excellence, let them do it and hire staff persons with gifts in other areas. If no one is capable of leading worship with excellence, this is so crucial to reaching and keeping people that it warrants hiring a staff person with expertise in this area.

The danger many churches face is the tendency to pile on staff in the discipleship and congregational care areas while neglecting the outreach, evangelism, and assimilation side of the equation. Before adding more people to work with youth, children, men's ministries, women's ministries, and pastoral care, stop and evaluate: Who is reaching and keeping new people?

Without thinking this through, many churches have staffed themselves right into a plateau or even a decline. In our mobile society, with families moving every few years, a church has to keep reaching new people just to replace those who transfer out of the area. Factor in losses due to death, illness, and other reasons

Priorities in Hiring

If the senior pastor is gifted on this side of the continuum, then . . . | . . . hire the second staff person to fill one of the roles on this side.

Finding People	Keeping People	Celebrating with People	Educating People	Overseeing People	Caring for People

Hire the second staff person to fill one of the roles on this side if . . . | . . . the senior pastor is gifted on this side of the continuum.

Finding People	Keeping People	Celebrating with People	Educating People	Overseeing People	Caring for People

—Gary L. McIntosh

why people quit coming to church, and the numbers begin to slide. Somebody has to pay attention to outreach.

When hiring staff persons, McIntosh recommends alternating between the two sides, which may generally be described as outreach and pastoral care. Alternating keeps the church from falling into the trap of loading too many staff people on one side of the equation. All outreach will weaken the church's pastoral care. Too many staff in pastoral care will cut off the influx and incorporation of new people.

Restructuring for Growth

What are some other practical considerations in restructuring the church for growth and expansion?

Preparing the Congregation

A pastor needs to prepare his congregation for staff expansion. We can't assume that everyone will understand the need for more staff. We can't assume they will immediately accept and embrace new staff persons. We can't assume they'll cooperate with new staff.

Showing the need involves helping people understand both the urgency of the Great Commission and the limitations of current staff. Every church has a mandate to reach as many people as possible. No one gets a pass on stopping at any point and saying, "The church is large enough."

Years ago, Stuart Briscoe told an audience about a conversation he had with a parishioner whom he met in a grocery store. The church of which Briscoe was pastor had about six hundred attendees at the time. The parishioner said, "The church is big enough. Six hundred people are enough for any church."

Briscoe answered, "Why do you think six hundred is enough?"

"It's just understood. That's enough for any church," said the man.

"Well, I certainly don't understand it," said Briscoe. "I have read a fairly good book on church growth, the book of Acts, and at last count there were five thousand men, not counting the women and children. Later it says the number of disciples in Jerusalem increased rapidly, so we really don't know how many there were, but it exceeded five thousand."

Most of us have a long way to go to reach our potential. Yet a solo pastor is limited in the number of people he can minister to and still be effective. So our rationale for growing includes the fact that the Great Commission demands it and our human limitations dictate we need help.

Getting Approval

Who needs to give approval to the hiring of staff? Different church disciplines may include a variety of ways it can be handled. Most pastors do not have carte blanche in hiring staff. A local board of administration, a board of elders, or a church council will have something to say about it in most cases. Some churches may also have a personnel committee that will want to have input.

Whatever the procedure, the pastor must secure approval. In fact, pastors are smart if they secure board approval before they approach the congregation about it. In more congregational churches, the constituency may actually vote on who is hired. In many cases, a board represents the congregation in giving approval for hiring.

As in any matter of major importance, it's wise to have "the meeting
before the meeting." A lunch or breakfast meeting with influential leaders,
either together or one at a time, can
save a pastor major headaches. If your

Shared Leadership

Leadership is not something you do to people; it's something you do with them.

—Ken Blanchard

top influencer is opposed to the idea of staffing, you ought to know that before you take it to the board. A private discussion is much better than a public confrontation.

Input from your laypeople is vital. Those who are kingdom-minded want the church to grow. They also want to save their senior pastor from burnout. They may see your limitations in sharper focus than you do. Many senior pastors suffer from the "super pastor" syndrome (see Chapter 10). A wise layperson will defend you against those who think the church does not need additional staff.

Board members may be reluctant for a variety of reasons. Some may be concerned about what it's going to cost the church. Others may think that if you were really putting in the time you should be spending for the church, the work would get done without additional help. Others may simply lack a vision for growth and expansion.

A loyal layperson who understands the rationale for expanding staff and is enthusiastic about church growth can be a zealous ally to help you sell your vision to the board. Such a person can multiply your chances of winning approval because he or she is speaking on your behalf, yet without your personal bias.

Restructuring the Budget

In Chapter 2 we talked about funding your staffing plan. Here we want to highlight again the importance of thinking through your decision to hire from an economic standpoint. This is where you have to sharpen your pencil and do the calculations as accurately as possible so you do not make a mistake about what it costs to add staff.

Think through every nuance: the cost of bringing candidates for interviews, moving costs, what it will take to furnish another office, and we haven't even gotten to salary and benefits yet. If you are hiring a full-time person, you must think through what it will take for that person to live in your community. What about housing? What does it cost to rent or buy in your community? What other benefits will you offer?

You may want to take a survey of comparable churches in your community. Find out what they are paying and what benefits they offer. Discover what is standard in your denomination. Can you match the compensation others are providing? We don't like to think we are in competition with other churches, but in many ways we are. We need to be competitive without having a competitive spirit.

Who's Running the Church?

The pastor of a large church told Fred Smith he was going to Africa with his staff. Fred asked how many he was going to take. The pastor said, "All of them. All the personnel—eleven ministers."

Fred asked, "Who's going to run the church?

He answered, "The same laypeople who are running it when we're here."[6]

Fred makes the point that this pastor understood his job was to minister to people, not simply to run the church. He had been successful in bringing his church to the point where lay leadership and staff leadership worked in such tandem that the staff could be gone for a few weeks without the ministry of the church missing a beat.

We're not all at that point yet. On the other hand, I hope we are not still at the Mom-and-Pop stage. The maximum efficiency of the multiple staff church that can send its full staff on a missions trip may be the ideal toward which to strive. The Mom-and-Pop operation is the other extreme we must conscientiously avoid.

With zeal and passion, we must move in the direction of delegating to laypersons what we can. Then when the time comes to hire staff, we will carefully restructure the church to accommodate that kind of ministry.

Action Steps

1. What are your gifts as a senior pastor? (If you are reading this as a layperson, what are your senior pastor's dominant gifts?) What gifts should you look for in the next staff person you hire? Think through what gaps you want to cover.

2. What gifted people in your congregation are being underutilized? How can you involve them for maximum effectiveness?

9

RECRUITMENT
Finding and Hiring the Right Person

Finding the right people is like mining for gold.

The gold rush of '29 caused a great deal of excitement in some quarters. It preceded the famous "Forty-Niners" gold rush in California by two decades. The "Twenty-Niners" rushed, not west, but south! Northern Georgia was their destination. The hills of Lumpkin County near Dahlonega attracted miners from all across the nation, as well as from European countries, in 1829 and the years that followed.

> Your goal in hiring is to get the right players on the field. Luckily, great people are everywhere. You just have to know how to pick them.
>
> —Jack Welch

Determined miners panned, sluiced, and dug for gold. Some were farmers or had other occupations and mined only part time. Mining operations in Georgia declined in the 1840s and many miners went west, attracted by the California gold rush of 1849. Georgia mining waxed and waned through the remainder of the nineteenth century and even into the mid-twentieth century.

The Smith House in Dahlonega, Georgia, still thrives as a historic landmark and a place where travelers may enjoy a bed and a meal. If you like fried chicken, sweet baked ham, roast beef, fried okra, and candied yams, you can get it all at the Smith House.

In 2006, when the structure underwent some renovation, workers dug through the floor of the main dining room and discovered the entrance to an old gold mine. Warren Lamb cites a legend that declares Captain Frank Hall, who built the house in the 1890s, discovered gold and wanted to mine it on that site. The city fathers refused, according to the legend, partly because it was too close to the downtown square and partly because he was a Yankee. It appears he built the house over the mine and continued the operation anyway. Current owners have been quoted as saying they were literally sitting on a gold mine.[1]

Senior pastors who want to expand their staff are hoping to find gold when they go prospecting for associates to join them in ministry.

Andrew Carnegie employed forty-three millionaires in the 1930s, during the height of the depression. Someone asked him how he had managed to attract and hire so many millionaires. He replied that they weren't millionaires when he hired them.

When someone pressed him to reveal how he developed these individuals into persons of wealth, he replied, "Men are developed the same way gold is mined. Several tons of dirt must be moved to get an ounce of gold. But you don't go into the mine looking for dirt. You go in looking for gold."[2]

Hopeful senior pastors are looking for gold as well, hidden in valuable personalities and skills. Prospective staff persons are out there, some working in other churches, some still sharpening their axes in college and seminary, and some ministering as volunteers right under the senior pastors' noses.

Prospecting for Gold

Gold is not always easy to find. Brian Cavanaugh tells about a great gold discovery near Cripple Creek, Colorado. It seems gold and the mineral tellurium occur together in tellurite ore, but early refining methods were inadequate to separate one from the other. A miner picked up a chunk of the ore, thinking it was coal, and tossed it in his stove. Later, when removing ashes from the stove, he found sediments of pure gold in the bottom. The heat had burned away the tellurium, leaving pure gold. Workers found a way to refine the ore and the discovery led to a fortune.[3]

Pastors face many challenges in prospecting for staff persons, not unlike the difficulty in separating gold from the tellurite ore. Todd Rhoades asked a group of pastors their opinion as to how church staffing has changed over recent years. Most of them declared, "There's no problem finding candidates for a position. The problem is finding *qualified* candidates who meet the requisites for the job and are a good fit for your church."[4]

In other words, it's the challenge of finding where the gold is hidden. Specifically, here are some of the concerns pastors face.

Finding Quality Persons

Some pastors find people who have the right educational background but who do not have good people skills. Others don't have confidence in the skills they do have.

One pastor tells about an associate, recently graduated from seminary, who faced the challenge of calling on a newly diagnosed cancer patient. He balked, saying, "My training didn't prepare me for this!"

On the one hand, how can anyone get through seminary without facing the reality of dealing with life-threatening diseases? On the other hand, how can anyone ever be fully prepared to deal with people who have been told they are probably going to die sooner than expected? None of us

Aiming Too Low

The greater danger for most of us lies not in setting our aim too high and falling short, but in setting our aim too low, and achieving our mark.

—Michelangelo

is prepared unless we depend on the Holy Spirit for wisdom and discretion in approaching many situations. Yet, if we're called into the ministry, how can we dodge these tasks, difficult though they are?

Ray Brock, a pastor in Ohio, nailed the problem many potential staffers have, when he observed that "biblical knowledge and willingness does not equal a good staff member. It seems that many candidates are not aware of the definition of *commitment*. Many candidates have the skills but they lack in character, good decision-making skills, and the pursuit of holiness."[5]

The Internet Is Your Friend—or Not!

Internet sites are springing up to make the senior pastor's job easier. Sites such as ChurchStaffing.com, Pastorfinder.com, and ChurchJobs.net offer shortcuts in accessing the resumes of staffers who are looking for new opportunities. Yet does that make the job any easier?

Ron Hand, a pastor in Georgia, says, "It is easier than ever to let others know about your position, but with an abundance of responses, it is harder to make decisions."[6]

With the Internet, a senior pastor can have instant access to dozens of resumes from all over the nation. Yet this does not always make the job easier.

We've already mentioned the search committee chair who called a district supervisor and said, "I just downloaded nineteen resumes from the Internet. May I distribute these to the committee?"

"Whoa!" the supervisor said. "Send them to me first!"

In his denomination, the district superintendent serves as a clearing house or quality control person to check credentials, theological persuasions, and whether a candidate might be a good fit for a particular church. In this particular case, the chair soberly narrowed the field to two resumes and sent those to the district supervisor for his approval.

Hire Inside or Outside?

Increasing numbers of churches have practiced hiring persons from within their congregations instead of looking outside the church and the community to find new staff members. This practice, while more popular than ever, has both advantages and disadvantages.

Advantages

- The senior pastor already knows the layperson he hires; having observed his or her personality, temperament, and work habits.
- New associates hired from within the church bring with them a network of friends, relatives, and associates that may make recruiting for ministries somewhat easier.
- A person from within is already committed to the senior pastor's vision; otherwise that person would likely not already be involved.

Disadvantages

- New hires may or may not be prepared to deal with the "underbelly of the church." They will be exposed to problems and problem people as never before. They'll soon begin to realize that even church staff members don't deserve to be on a pedestal.
- A person hired internally may be difficult to fire. That network of friends, relatives, and associates mentioned above may rally around a dismissed staff member and create a body of antagonism toward the senior pastor who let their friend go.
- Persons from within may not have professional training for the work they're hired to do. If they have sufficient experience, that may not be a problem. Sending them to seminars can add to their level of expertise.

You Can't Be Too Careful

Years ago, a senior pastor called his friends, worked his network of acquaintances, solicited resumes, talked to a few people, prayed about the selection of a candidate, and hired the best person he could find. Now some churches have a mandatory policy of conducting a criminal background on all candidates.

We've learned through painful experience that it's best to ask a few probing questions while doing our reference checking than to assume the best and be disappointed later. It's good to find out as much about the candidate as possible. How does a candidate treat his or her spouse? How does the spouse treat the candidate? What level of support for the candidate's ministry does the spouse seem to have? How do they interact with their children?

Change

Everyone thinks of changing the world, but no one thinks of changing himself.

—Leo Tolstoy

One senior pastor tells about checking the references for an associate. In his fourth or fifth reference, he asked, "Is there any other question I should have asked?" The reference was honest enough to reveal the prospective staff member had a history of abusing his wife. This was not something any other reference had addressed, even though some would have known about this problem. It pays to be careful.

A Divine Strategy for Staff Selection

Wouldn't it be fascinating to know how Jesus knew whom to choose as his twelve apostles? Even a surface reading of the gospels shows us that none of them was perfect. Peter was impulsive. James and John had anger control problems; why else were they called "sons of thunder"? Thomas wavered in his faith. Judas betrayed his Lord. Andrew led various people to Jesus, but with all his commendable qualities, didn't make the "big three"—Peter, James, and John—who comprised the "inner circle" and were with Jesus on occasions when the others were not.

Prayer—an Integral Part

One clue we have to his decision-making strategy is found in Luke's gospel:

> One of those days Jesus went out to a mountainside to pray, and spent the night praying to God. When morning came, he called his disciples to him and chose twelve of them, whom he also designated apostles: Simon (whom he named Peter), his brother Andrew, James, John, Philip, Bartholomew, Matthew, Thomas, James son of Alphaeus, Simon who was called the Zealot, Judas son of James, and Judas Iscariot, who became a traitor (Luke 6:12–16).

While prayer is not the only thing we do, it ought to be the first thing we do. Further, as Pat MacMillan states, "Prayer is not just the first step of a process, but rather an integral part of every step."[7]

Ken Heer suggests that Jesus prayed, "knowing the critical nature of choosing in whom He would invest His life, . . . knowing what those He chose would have to face because of their commitment to follow Him," and "knowing the choice of the Twelve would launch Him into a new phase of His ministry."[8]

If Jesus felt the need to spend all night in prayer before choosing his closest associates, how much more do we need to pray? To neglect such a strategy is unwise. The wise man said, "Like an archer who wounds at random is he who hires a fool or any passer-by" (Prov. 26:10). By sincere prayer, we can avoid this folly.

Moses and Samuel Prayed

Jesus is not the only leader to employ the strategy of prayer. Moses did so hundreds of years earlier when he knew he could not lead the people into the Promised Land. He pleaded with God to raise up a new leader: "May the LORD, the God of the spirits of all mankind, appoint a man over this community to go out and come in before them, one who will lead them out and bring them in, so the LORD's people will not be like sheep without a shepherd" (Num. 27:16–17).

God answered that prayer and elevated Joshua to the position of leader.

Samuel, when seeking a new king of Israel, depended on God for direction. The historical record does not say he specifically prayed about the process. The Bible does tell us that he and God had a conversation, first about God's rejection of Saul, the first king of Israel. Then God told Samuel to go to Bethlehem and anoint a new king.

In a wonderful example of the power of the Holy Spirit to guide a person in a given situation, God directed Samuel away from Eliab, impressive-looking firstborn of Jesse. Eventually God instructed Samuel to anoint David, the chosen one of God, to be the next king of Israel.

The story seems to teach us that prayer is the essential ingredient, both before and during the selection process.

New Testament Examples of Prayer

The apostles utilized the strategy of prayer. After the demise of Judas Iscariot, they met together and proposed two men—Joseph and Matthias. Luke records: "Then they prayed, 'Lord, you know everyone's heart. Show us which of these two you have chosen to take over this apostolic ministry'" (Acts 1:24–25).

After the prayer, they chose Matthias.

When Paul left Titus on the island of Crete, he gave him this challenge: "The reason I left you in Crete was that you might straighten out what was left unfinished and appoint elders in every town, as I directed you" (Titus 1:5).

We do not read in the short letter to Titus whether Paul admonished his protégé to pray about his selection. We do know Paul gave him a list of qualities to look for in the potential leaders he chose (Titus 1:6–9). Knowing his mentor's approach to problems, we may assume that Titus approached the process prayerfully, not only asking for specific guidance but also praying for wisdom and insight.

Finding the Right People

Some observers see a developing trend in church staff. Often pastors are finding potential staff persons who view ministry as a profession rather than a calling.[9] How can senior pastors be sure they're hiring the right people who will commit to ministry as a calling and not just a profession?

Getting the Right People on the Bus

Author and professor Jim Collins places great emphasis on "getting the right people on the bus,"[10] which is what every senior pastor wants to do. First, he says, begin with *who* rather than *what* if you want to adapt to a changing world. In other words, it's more important to get the right people involved with the right people than to get them on the bus for other reasons. When you need to change direction, they will remain loyal because they are loyal to the team, not because they are committed to a certain direction.

Second, Collins believes motivation is less of a problem when you have the right people on the bus. The right people are self-motivated because they want to produce the best results. You don't have to manage them tightly or ride herd on them when they have an inner drive to be part of creating something great.

Internal motivation is a powerful thing. Wayne Jacobsen tells the story of Rees Howells, a Welsh coal miner who became an intercessor. During one period of his life, Rees walked two miles each way to lead a Bible study in a distant village. Every night. After a twelve-hour day in the mines.

One night he came home completely soaked after walking through a downpour. When his father saw him, the older man said, "I wouldn't have walked across there tonight for twenty pounds."

"Nor would I for twenty pounds," answered Rees.[11]

It wasn't about getting paid. It was about doing the right thing with the right people. While we want to compensate our staff persons as generously as we can, this is the kind of internal motivation we desire in our associates.

Third, it doesn't matter whether you're heading in the right direction if you have the wrong people on the bus. The wrong people won't help you reach your destination, no matter what it is. As Collins says, "Great vision without great people is irrelevant."[12]

Ingredients for Finding Quality People

Dr. C. Peter Wagner suggests three vital ingredients to finding quality staff persons.[13] First, we should recruit staff on the basis of their spiritual gifts. Even as Samuel had to learn the lesson that God does not look on the outward appearance, but looks on the heart (1 Sam. 16:7), we must learn that an impressive resume, a handsome or beautiful appearance, and a good personality are not the prime considerations. Instead, look for a good match regarding spiritual gifts. If the position involves a great deal of administration, don't hire someone who has no administrative gifts, no matter how many other positions he or she has held.

Second, recruit potential staff members on the basis of their loyalty to the senior pastor. Respect and loyalty must be earned, of course, so how will you know prior to hiring how loyal that person will be? In your reference-checking, you can probe as to attitudes toward authority, respect for supervision, and cooperation with the overseer's direction. A person with a good track record in this area is more likely to be loyal than one who has had issues with authority.

Loyalty

You can buy a man's time; you can buy his physical presence at a given place; you can even buy a measured number of his skilled muscular motions per hour. But you cannot buy enthusiasm . . . you cannot buy loyalty . . . you cannot buy the devotion of hearts, minds, or souls. You must earn those.

—Clarence Francis

Third, Wagner suggests you hire new staff members who'll buy into the church's philosophy of ministry. If your church is heavily into outreach, you won't want to hire staff persons who criticize your evangelistic methods. If you're heavily into small groups, you don't want to hire those who see no value in this strategy.

Locating People of Value

At first glance, you might be tempted to criticize that heading—"people of value." After all, every person is an individual of inestimable worth. When you consider that Jesus died on the cross for every person on the planet, it is obvious that God sees us as persons of worth. Jesus said, "What good will it be for a man if he gains the whole world, yet forfeits his soul? Or what can a man give in exchange for his soul?" (Matt. 16:26). Who can place a dollar amount on the value of an individual?

But what I'm talking about here is the value that people bring to the positions for which you hire them. Will they add value to the church? To the ministry they will oversee? To the people with whom they will minister?

Earlier in this book, I addressed such qualities as character, competence, and compatibility. To find the right people, you must look for persons with such qualities. You also must find people who will add value and in whom you want to invest.

Several years ago, the Smithsonian Institution's National Museum of American History in Washington, D.C., undertook the project of restoring "The Star Spangled Banner." This famous flag inspired Francis Scott Key to write our national anthem in 1814.

A year earlier, Lt. Col. George Armistead, commander of Fort McHenry, Maryland, commissioned Mary Pickersgill to make the new flag. It originally measured thirty feet by forty-two feet and cost the U.S. Army $405.90.

The project to restore the flag took three years of surgery-like precision in a specially designed laboratory and cost $18 million. Why would the National Museum of American History spend so much money on this project? Clearly, the museum directors believe "there are some things, indeed many things, worth preserving."[14]

The right people are worth your investment as senior pastor. They're worth your time, your training, and your involvement, because they will in turn extend your ministry by adding value to those with whom they minister.

Who Are the Right People?

It's not wise to drive down the highway, constantly looking in the rearview mirror. You have to pay attention to where you're going. Have you ever noticed, though, that life often makes more sense when you look in the rearview mirror? We seem to understand life better by analyzing what happened, what we did, and what others did, than we do in trying to forecast what will happen, what they will say, or what they will do.

This is why, in getting to know people, we ask questions about what they did in the past. How did they behave in a given situation? What did they do when faced with certain obstacles? We do this because we believe past behavior is usually an accurate predictor of future performance. Not always, of course.

People can change. They can learn from their mistakes. If they don't, they're apt to repeat them.

There's no way to guarantee our prospective associates won't fail. Not even Jesus guaranteed that. And look at his method of choosing the disciples. He was not careless. As Bill Hybels observed, "He didn't just say, 'Here's a line. First twelve guys that step across it get picked.' No, he selected his disciples carefully. He took his time and prayed fervently before he chose them."[15]

Yet, even though Jesus chose his followers with deliberate care, Judas betrayed him, Peter denied him, and all the apostles fled in an hour of crisis (Matt. 26:56).

To the best of our ability, then, after checking people's history, here's what we look for in potential staff persons.

Love for God

If they're going to be automobile mechanics, this isn't a prerequisite. A farmer could be successful, even if he is an atheist. You could tune pianos and not be a believer in God. But not the staff person in your church—that person must love God. Christian workers must do the work they do because their primary loyalty is to Christ, who loved them and gave himself for them.

The work is too hard and the compensation is too small to do it for any other primary reason.

Love for People

Christian workers have various levels of involvement with people. Some draw energy from spending time with people. Others find their energy drained after a great deal of people interaction. Yet everyone in God's work must believe in his children, care about them, and be devoted to adding value to others.

A few Christian workers I have known are like the little girl who came home from church one Sunday after sitting in the adult worship service with her parents.

At dinner, she informed them, "When I grow up, I want to be like the man up front."

"You want to be a minister?" her father asked.

"No," she answered, "I just want to tell people what to do."

Working with People

Many candidates are professionally qualified for tasks. However, many candidates are lacking in the ability to work well with others.

—Todd Rhoades

That's not a worthy motive. We're looking for staff members who want to invest in others, encourage others, and add value to others. All of us need to love people and believe in them, like Robert H. Schuller's uncle Henry believed in him.

On a dusty summer day Uncle Henry, fresh from missionary service in China, arrived at the Schuller farm in northwest Iowa. Barefoot Robert stood on the front porch and watched his handsome uncle get out of the car and walk up to the house. Henry put both his hands on Robert's four-year-old shoulders and said, "Well! I guess you're Robert! I think you're going to be a preacher someday!"

That night young Robert prayed, "And dear God, make me a preacher when I grow up!" Schuller believes God made him a possibility thinker then and there.[16]

Not all of us will accomplish what Schuller has done. But we and our staffers can all be encouragers of others who may accomplish great things. We need to be lovers of people.

A Great Work Ethic

People who are not very energetic can try to hide in the ministry. Many have. The typical solo pastor does not punch a time clock, has large amounts of discretionary time with no one looking over his shoulder, and, with a little effort, can give an appearance of achievement while barely getting by.

This is more difficult for staff persons, because they usually have an immediate supervisor. They report to the senior pastor, who monitors their progress and assesses their work. Yet even staff persons can coast, especially if the senior pastor is not attentive. They can drift and maintain ministry rather than putting forth creative effort to excel.

Pope John possessed an admirable sense of humor. A report asked him how many people worked in the Vatican. He answered, "About half of them!"[17]

Andrew Carnegie observed, "The average person puts twenty-five percent of his energy and ability into his work. The world takes off its hat to those who put in more than fifty percent of their capacity, and stands on its head for those few and far between souls who devote one hundred percent."

> **With All Your Heart**
>
> Whatever you do, work at it with all your heart, as working for the Lord, not for men. . . . It is the Lord Christ you are serving.
>
> —Paul

Blessed is the pastor who finds staff people who love God, love people, and have a great work ethic. Find individuals who have sterling character, outstanding competence, and compatibility with your vision and the church's mission. It takes extra work, but such persons are worth finding.

A Gem Worth Finding

Ten-year-old Lawrence Shields found a treasure in North Carolina in 1995. While picking through a bucket of debris in a gemstone mine, he spotted a rock that he particularly liked. "I just liked the shape of it," he said.

He brushed the dirt off the rock and rubbed it on his shirt to polish it up a bit. He began to think it was more than an ordinary rock. Sure enough, it turned about to be a sapphire. Not your ordinary, run-of-the-mill gemstone either. It was a 1,061-carat sapphire.[18]

What a discovery! When you find the right people and they turn out to exceed your expectations, it's like finding a sapphire. Or gold. It's worth all the time and effort it took to be sure you hired correctly in the first place.

Action Steps

1. Make a list of potential staff members, even if you aren't ready to hire. When you are ready, or should they become available, you will have given it some thought.

2. List the qualities of the person you are likely to need in your next hire. Whom do you know that might fill this need?

3. What layperson currently serving in your church might have what it takes to become a hired staff person? Would part-time fit their schedule better while still meeting the church's needs?

10

ATTITUDE
Overcoming the Super Pastor Syndrome

*Ministers who don't overcome the
Super Pastor Syndrome limit their effectiveness.*

Pastor Clark had barely finished saying grace when his cell phone rang. Grabbing it from his belt and flipping it open, he listened for a couple of moments, then snapped it shut and rose from the table.

> Jesus invested everything he had in a team. The Bible knows nothing of solo ministry, only team ministry.
>
> —Leonard Sweet[1]

"Mrs. Grant is going in for x-rays," he said while striding toward the bedroom.

"Can't it wait until after dinner?" his wife Lois asked.

"Nope. Gotta run. It's my responsibility."

Turning back to the children, Lois urged them to finish their meals.

Meanwhile, in the bedroom, Pastor Clark spun rapidly at the foot of the bed. His ordinary clothes went flying and when he stopped, he paused only a moment, catching a glimpse of his red and blue uniform in the vanity mirror. He leaped to the window, pulled it open, and jumped out, cape billowing in the breeze.

He gained altitude and cleared the trees in his neighborhood. As he streaked across the sky, heading for the hospital on the other side of town, pedestrians looked up as they heard the sound of a mighty rushing wind.

"Look! Up in the sky!"

"It's a bird!"

"It's a plane!"

"No, it's Super Pastor!"

Landing gracefully on the hospital roof, Pastor Clark opened the door leading the top floor. He bounded down the stairs and found Mrs. Grant's room, having scanned the entire eight floors of the hospital with his x-ray vision while he was coming in for a landing.

"Oh, Super Pastor, how good of you to come!" Mrs. Grant exclaimed when he walked through the door. "I don't know how I could face these x-rays without you!"

"It's the least I could do," he responded, taking her hand and offering one of his super prayers before rushing back across the night sky to the church. He arrived just in time to lead the opening prayer for the Sunday school staff meeting.

All in an evening's work as he kept his commitment to truth, justice, and the Christian way!

Unknown to Pastor Clark, lurking in his bodily systems, are a super case of ulcers and a super episode of burnout, waiting for the right time to engulf him in a super breakdown. And that doesn't begin to deal with the super ticked-off wife waiting for him at home.

Like many pastors, Clark has not learned to delegate. He hasn't learned to trust others with ministry. A staff is very far from his thoughts, except for an unrealistic wish that he didn't have to do it all. The wish is unrealistic because he won't let go of anything. He has to have his fingers in every pie. He hasn't learned that he can move beyond doing ministry to seeing that ministry is done.

Stuck in a Rut

Why do pastors want to do it all themselves? Why would they not want to enlist others in order to be more effective, to prevent burnout, and to expand their years of usefulness to the kingdom?

A few pastors may be stuck in small churches where there seem to be no other leaders or potential leaders. But far more pastors are their own worst enemies. They hurt themselves because of their own negative attitudes.

Lack of Trust

Are you a Super Pastor who hasn't learned to trust others? Are you afraid they'll make mistakes? Are you afraid they won't perform to your standard? Let me assure you, they will make mistakes and their performance may not always rise to your standard.

But consider this: Peter denied Jesus. When the crisis came, Peter failed the test. Yet Jesus forgave him and entrusted him with a huge ministry: "Feed my sheep," Jesus told him (John 21:17).

David committed adultery with Bathsheba and paid for his sin many times over. Yet the Scripture calls him a man after God's heart (Acts 13:22).

Samson fell into sexual sin with Delilah, yet God restored him and listed him as one of the champions of the faith (Heb. 11:32).

Others may disappoint you, but on the whole, I have found staff to be anxious to do a good job, to honor God, and contribute to the health of the church. Learn to trust others.

Pride

Super Pastors have problems with ego. From their perspective, nobody can do it as well, as fast, or with the thoroughness of the Super Pastor.

A friend who was elected to one of the top jobs in his denomination looked around the room at a site where he was to give a major address. Plastered on the door to one of the exits was the sign: "Caution! Large step down!"

> **A Big Step**
>
> It marks a big step in your development when you come to realize that other people can help you do a better job than you could do alone.
>
> —Andrew Carnegie

It hit him with full force that, while it's an honor to have a high position, if we don't handle it well, it can be a large step down! No wonder the wise man said, "First pride, then the crash—the bigger the ego, the harder the fall" (Prov. 16:18 MSG).

Before we crash, we need to learn to trust others and depend on their contributions.

Cynicism

It's easy to become cynical. When you decide to trust someone with a task and they let you down, it's easy to think, "I'll never do that again. It's better if I do it myself."

In worst-case scenarios, those we trust do not simply let us down. They betray us. Or criticize us. Or blame us.

Mike Murdock points out, "Betrayal is external. Bitterness is internal. Betrayal is something that others do to you. Bitterness is something you do to yourself."[2]

So guard against bitterness, which can lead to cynicism. Like getting back on the proverbial bicycle, we have to trust others, even though they sometimes disappoint us.

Weak Leadership

Few people are born leaders. Not many of us have had fathers like Bill Hybels' dad. He told Bill from the time he was a little guy that he was a leader. Bill's father would throw him into all kinds of challenging, high-risk situations. Then he would say, "You're a leader. You'll figure it out."[3]

Most of us have not had fathers who pushed us into leadership. Most of us have to develop qualities of leadership as we go along through life.

Here are some factors that contribute to making our leadership weak.

Insecurity. Pastors who don't develop a team of supporting players in the church may be afraid someone else will do a better job and overshadow their own performance. Or an insecure pastor may be afraid to relinquish control over some aspect of the work.

On the other hand, a secure pastor makes a better leader. "The most effective leaders are not afraid to help others reach their goals; they believe in the power of the win-win situation."[4]

Indecision. An indecisive pastor cannot make up his mind about whether to have staff, what kind of staff the church needs, or how best to use staff to accomplish the church's mission.

Leaders learn to be decisive. A poor decision-maker may not understand, as Ralph Waldo Emerson stated, "Once you make a decision, the universe conspires to make it happen."

Inexperience. Some pastors have never participated in a healthy staff relationship. Don Cousins observed, "Many church leaders bear incredible loads because they haven't mastered the art of raising up fellow leaders and releasing responsibility to them."[5]

Decision

Decision is a sharp knife that cuts clean and straight; indecision is a dull one that hacks and tears and leaves ragged edges behind.

– Gordon Graham

My friend Ron told me his first senior pastor was inexperienced; Ron was the first paid staff person with whom the minister had ever worked. When Ron became a senior pastor, his earlier experience enabled him to do a better job than he might have done otherwise. He had learned both how to do it and how not to do it from his senior pastor.

We have all had bad experiences. The challenge is to learn from them, not be permanently scarred by them.

Lack of Vision

I addressed the need for vision in Chapter 1, so I won't labor the point here. Lack of vision is a factor as to why some pastors never develop a staff ministry. Their Super Pastor Syndrome will not permit them to think in those terms. They haven't learned what Henrietta Mears discovered: "There is no magic in small plans. When I consider my ministry, I think of the world.

Anything less than that would not be worthy of Christ nor of His will for my life."

If senior pastors want to increase their ministry impact on the world beyond their churches, they must learn to develop a greater vision for working through others.

Jesus Invested in Others

Jesus could have been the ultimate Super Pastor. He could have done it all himself. Instead he called twelve apostles to be with him as he performed itinerant ministry in Galilee, Samaria, and Judea. By looking at how he treated and trained others, we may pick up some clues about effective ministry as a team, thus avoiding the Super Pastor Syndrome.

Jesus Called Others

Jesus could have preached to the multitudes by himself. He could have healed the sick alone. He could have died on a cross without anyone to mourn his death. Instead he chose to invest himself in the lives of others.

As Jesus walked along the shore of the Sea of Galilee, he saw two brothers, Simon Peter and Andrew, busy performing their duties as fishermen. He interrupted their net-casting and said to them, "Come, follow me, and I will make you fishers of men" (Matt. 4:19). They abandoned their nets and followed Jesus.

A short time later, he encountered two more fishermen who were also brothers. James and John were preparing their nets with their father, Zebedee. Jesus interrupted them as well, with an invitation to follow him. They abandoned their boat and their father and followed Jesus.

Jesus Developed Others

When he called the disciples, it was for more than fellowship, although he enjoyed their company. His goal was to develop them, disciple them, and train them in how to follow him and how to lead others.

He taught them about prayer (Matt. 26:36–46). He taught them about heaven (John 14:2–4). He taught them about hell (Luke 16:19–31). He taught in the synagogues (Luke 13:10). He taught in the villages (Mark 6:6).

We too need to develop those with whom we work. Our staff "may not see what you see. They may not feel what you feel. They may not have discovered what you know. You must invest time to nurture their vision."[6]

Jesus Empowered Others

We see how secure Jesus was in that he empowered others to do the work he could have done more quickly and with greater expertise than they did. He sent disciples to arrange for a meal in the Upper Room. He sent them to secure a donkey on which to ride into Jerusalem. Even more significant was his decision to entrust them with ministry. He told them, "I tell you the truth, anyone who has faith in me will do what I have been doing. He will do even greater things than these, because I am going to the Father" (John 14:12).

One of our greatest historical examples of empowerment is Abraham Lincoln. Our sixteenth president did the unthinkable.

He filled several cabinet posts with men who had been his political rivals. Edwin M. Stanton had treated Lincoln with contempt when the two men were involved in a celebrated law case in the summer of 1855. Yet Lincoln chose him to be secretary of war, the most powerful civilian post of the day.

Salmon P. Chase felt *he* deserved the presidency and ran against Lincoln prior to the Republican Convention of 1860. Yet Lincoln appointed him secretary of the treasury.

William H. Seward, a renowned senator and governor from the state of New York, was certain *he* would become president. When Lincoln appointed him secretary of state, Seward fancied himself as more powerful than the president. He underestimated Lincoln's prowess and eventually became one of his closest friends and allies.

Edward Bates enjoyed a wide respect as a statesman from Missouri. He too ran against Lincoln in 1860 and lost. He intended to reject a cabinet post if one were offered, but accepted the position of attorney general. Eventually he touted Lincoln as an unparalleled leader.

A lesser man would never have trusted his rivals. An insecure man would not have appointed them to his cabinet. But Lincoln did appoint them. In spite of the fact that they initially did not like him or each other, he made the arrangement work. He empowered others.

Jesus Deployed Others

Sending them out two by two, Jesus gave his followers careful instructions on how to behave and how to minister in various situations. When he sent out the Twelve, he "gave them authority over evil spirits" (Mark 6:7). When he sent out the seventy-two, he even said, "He who listens to you listens to me; he who rejects you rejects me" (Luke 10:16).

What extraordinary trust and confidence he displayed in them by deploying them to do the work of the ministry. When they returned, he debriefed them (Luke 10:17–20).

A senior pastor who learns to enjoy the success of his staff, instead of doing everything himself, is growing in maturity and wisdom as a leader. His own success is multiplied because more work is being accomplished as staff persons represent him and the church in their various areas of responsibility.

Jesus Trusted Others

With his limitations as a man, think how long it would have taken Jesus to distribute the loaves and fishes to five thousand people! So Jesus used wisdom and trusted his disciples with the task. After instructing his disciples to have the people sit down on the grass, he gave the apostles the loaves and fishes for distribution. Jesus had the satisfaction of watching them participate in ministry, and the disciples experienced the joy of being useful in the kingdom (Matt. 14:19)

I read somewhere that a businessman posted a sign on the wall of his office: "If I had to do it all over again, I'd ask someone to help me."

No Longer the Lone Ranger

Super Pastors are notorious for trying to do ministry alone. To change the metaphor, they try to be the Lone Ranger. Yet even the Lone Ranger did not ride alone. His faithful Indian companion Tonto was always at his side. Even so, it's an apt metaphor for what many pastors try to do and be.

As a kid, I used to hear episodes of *The Lone Ranger* on the radio. When those famous strains of the "William Tell Overture" escaped from the radio, we would gather around to hear the latest adventure of the masked man. Invariably he would get involved in someone's problem, calculate what needed to be done, outwit the bad guys, outdraw the fastest gun-slingers, outride the fastest horses on his renowned steed Silver, and eventually put the bad guys behind bars. If he ever did fall for some villain's plot, Tonto would find a way to rescue him.

Often, at the end of the story, he would leave a silver bullet, which was his trademark. As he rode off into the sunset, someone would ask, "Who was that masked man?" And some wise person would answer, "Why, that was the Lone Ranger."

It made for good entertainment, but life seldom works out just that way. People's problems are much too complicated to be analyzed and solved in thirty minutes. Yet some pastors maintain the delusion that they have the answers to all problems and can handle every situation without help from anyone. It's not only possible, they think, but it's expected. Any pastor worth his or her salt, they believe, is a generalist, who does it all and does it well.

In reality, we need others. We need a team. In smaller churches, volunteers comprise the team. As the church grows, we hire staff who will become a vital part of the teamwork it takes to do ministry well.

What are some principles to guide us in escaping the Super Pastor/Lone Ranger syndromes?

Develop an Unselfish Attitude

The work of the ministry is not about us as pastors. It's about Christ. It's about his Church and his people.

Put the ministry first. Many pastors' spouses may rise up at this point and say, "Yes, that's the problem! My husband puts the ministry first and the family gets whatever is left over, which usually isn't much."

I'm not making a plea for pastors to put the ministry before their families. We all must learn to balance ministry, family, and community and give each its priority at the right time.

What I'm talking about is being sure we don't make ministry about our personal success. It's about what's good for the church. The best pastors put the vision, mission, and objectives of the organization ahead of their own personalities and personal achievements.

Freely give credit to others. When you have staff, it's important to give them credit, both privately and pub

> **Whom We Hire**
>
> If each of us hires people who are smaller than we are, we shall become a company of dwarfs, but if each of us hires people who are bigger than we are, [we] will become a company of giants.
>
> —David Ogilvy

licly, when they do a good job. Let them know personally how much you appreciate what they do. Help them understand you value the contribution they make. Show them how they lighten your load, add value to the cause, and make the church's ministries better.

When it's appropriate, recognize them publicly. Tell the congregation how grateful you are for the staff's labors on behalf of the church.

Thank You

The first responsibility of a leader is to define reality. The last is to say thank you.

—Peter Drucker

When your staff looks good, you look good. You don't compliment them for this reason. But you're the leader, and when those you supervise do a good job, it reflects well on you. Your success together is good for the team and it's good for the church.

Learn to enjoy the success of others. Your vision for the church should be too big for you to accomplish alone. It should be such a great vision that it requires the efforts of many to make it happen. Recognize that others are a vital link in the chain of success.

When your staff excels, enjoy their success. When they stand in the spotlight and receive applause, be the biggest cheerleader. Be quick to celebrate it when they do a job well.

Develop a Team Mindset

Someone observed that one is too small a number to succeed. If you can succeed all by yourself, then your vision needs to grow. Gary L. McIntosh cites six keys that teams need in order to be effective.

Clear communication. Successful teams occur when members talk to each other. People have the freedom to express themselves without being criticized. Team members tolerate different points of view.

Shared goals. While each area of ministry may have its own goals, team members understand how their area fits into the total ministry of the church. When one area excels, others celebrate because it helps the whole church.

Collaborative atmosphere. Instead of being combative, successful teams members cooperate with each other. They collaborate and help one another, instead of being territorial and resenting others' success.

Responsibility and involvement. In a successful team, individual members take personal responsibility for their own areas, yet they stay involved with others. They're willing to help, support, cheer for, and encourage others on the team.

> **The Alternative**
>
> The alternative [to team ministry] is stagnancy, unnecessary frustration, and a future ministry that operates significantly below its God-given potential.
>
> —Dan Reeves

Flexible process. Unsuccessful teams tend to be rigid about their processes. They're not open to experimentation. Successful teams are more elastic and cooperative with others on the team.

Collegial support. Healthy teams see individual members as potential advisors or resource persons who are willing to give input as needed to assist others on the team. Rather than pursuing only individual goals, they care about the success of the group.[7]

Developing Your Staff

Senior pastors who spend time developing their staff will reap great rewards. Here are some ways to do it.

Spend Time with Them

I'm always amazed when I hear that pastoral staffs don't have regular meetings. Most successful staffs feel that a weekly meeting to report and share what's happening in each area is the minimum of what they need for good interaction.

In addition, a wise senior pastor spends individual time with each staff person who reports to him. In this way, the pastor and staff member get to know each other beyond superficial contact.

Social interaction is also important, when the conversation is not so much about work as it is about families, hobbies, and other things. Getting together with each other's families on occasion can also bond associates together.

Communicate with Them

E-mail is a blessing . . . and a curse. I have heard of senior pastors who communicated with staff only through e-mail, seldom face-to-face. This doesn't build healthy relationships.

A football team needs to know what the quarterback is planning. A ship's crew needs to know what the captain is thinking and where he plans to take the ship. Likewise, a church staff needs to have a good sense of the senior pastor's direction.

There are many ways to communicate, from group meetings to one-on-one interaction. There are many settings in which to communicate—the senior pastor's office, the associate's office, or some neutral location. But find a place and find a way to communicate regularly.

Support Them

Churches vary as to the amount of vacation time they grant for staff. Two weeks for hard-working staff persons hardly seems enough. Some judicatories specify the minimum vacation time for licensed personnel. A church is wise to err on the side of being more generous than too stingy with its vacation time.

A senior pastor should insist that his staff persons take their designated day off each week and should set the example by taking his own day off.

When staff persons and their families are going through difficult times, physically or emotionally, it means a great deal when the senior pastor is supportive. Granting time off to deal with emergencies or crises is a good practice.

Manage Conflicts

I almost called this section "Guard against conflicts," but the reality is that conflicts do come. They're almost unavoidable even in healthy staff situations. Seldom does a staff achieve perfect communication, for instance, without working hard at it. Failures in communicating with other staff members can lead to misunderstandings and even suspicion and distrust. So as senior pastor, encourage free-flowing communication between staff.

Other conflicts may arise if staff members become territorial and feel that other associates are infringing on their areas of responsibility. Or one staff member may solicit the help of other staff persons, which is healthy as long as it's occasional. If a staffer demands too much, associates may feel they are neglecting their responsibilities to assist a project that has gotten out of hand.

If staff members are having health problems or tensions at home, conflict may spill over into staff relationships. If a senior pastor is too controlling, conflicts may arise.

The lead pastor does not always need to solve every problem. Depending on the situation, you may want to encourage staff members to "work it out." In all cases, encourage good communication. Sometimes a healthy explanation will cause other staff members to realize there were elements to the problem they did not understand.

If you as lead pastor do have to get involved, deal with the issues and personalities as fairly as possible. Listening to both sides is a must. So is praying for wisdom. In every case, deal with the situation as soon as possible to keep attitudes from degenerating into full-blown resentment.

Reward Them

Rewards come in two categories: tangible and intangible. I have already addressed tangible rewards in Chapter 2 and in other places in this book. I alluded to intangible rewards above when I talked about giving credit and supporting staff.

What I want to add here is simply the importance of letting your staff know how important they are to the whole team and the whole ministry of the church. Celebrate every occasion you possibly can. When the church or the team reaches a milestone, celebrate. Use every excuse to cheer your team on to victory.

Life is Short

Pastor Clark bounded out of bed at two o'clock one morning, ready to shift into Super Pastor mode and fly off to the home of a parishioner having a heart attack. As he stood at the foot of the bed, ready to begin his famous spin, Lois woke up and said, "Clark, what are you doing? It's two o'clock in the morning."

Her voice cut through the fog in his brain and he looked down at his pajamas. Feeling foolish, he said, "I guess I was dreaming. I thought I was some kind of Super Pastor, ready to don a blue and red suit with a cape and fly across town to help a parishioner in need."

Lois yawned and said, "That wasn't a dream. That was a nightmare. Come back to bed."

As Clark crawled back under the covers, he thought about how foolish his dream was. Yet the reality was that he had been acting like he was a Super Pastor. He really did have an ulcer from trying to do it all.

No, he couldn't fly. He couldn't leap tall buildings in a single bound. And he wasn't more powerful than a speeding locomotive. He was just Clark. Sincere, hard-working, and conscientious. And ready to consider hiring staff. "Life is just too short," he thought, "to try to do everything myself."

Action Steps

1. What ministries could you release to someone else if you could find a competent, dedicated person to join you as an assistant pastor? Make a list and think about the qualities of the person you would need to handle those ministries.

2. If you currently have staff, how are you doing at "letting go" and letting them handle their areas of responsibility? What could you change that would improve both their performance and yours?

APPENDIX

Additional Resources

Chapter Five—Assessment
Twenty Questions to Ask Concerning the Candidate

1. Does the candidate have a vision for the church's ministry similar to that of the senior pastor and lay leaders?
2. Is the candidate's theological orientation similar to that of the senior pastor and lay leaders?
3. Does the candidate have a pattern of loyalty to the senior pastor and other individuals to whom he reports?
4. Does the candidate have ministry strengths that complement rather than duplicate those of the senior pastor and other key staff?
5. Does the candidate possess giftedness in the ministries that are major responsibilities in the job description?
6. Is the candidate a self-motivated self-starter?
7. Is the candidate dependable in delivering on promises and commitments?
8. Does the candidate usually follow through in completing administrative details?
9. Does the candidate have good interpersonal relationship skills?
10. Is the candidate a team player with other staff?

11. Is the candidate a person of honesty and integrity?
12. Is the candidate an effective time manger?
13. Is the candidate an effective conflict manager?
14. Does the candidate have a high energy level?
15. Does the candidate usually have a positive appearance?
16. Is the candidate sensitive to people's feelings and needs?
17. Is the candidate a good listener?
18. Is the candidate a clear communicator?
19. Is the candidate joyful and positive in conversation and manner?
20. Does the candidate possess spiritual enthusiasm and optimism?

—Herb Miller, "How to Select Additional Staff," *Net Results* XVII, no. 8 (August 1996), 8, cited by Gary McIntosh, *Staff Your Church for Growth* (Grand Rapids, Mich.: Baker, 2000).

Chapter Six—Retention
Performance Reviews

This form may be used for self-assessment as well as for objective assessment by supervisor.

Name: _____

Ministry Position: _____

Professional Performance

1. List the primary and secondary responsibilities of your job description and the percentage of time expended for each one.
2. Of these responsibilities, which one has been the most rewarding? Which one has been the most difficult? Explain.
3. What do you believe to be your single most effective area of expertise? How could the church make better use of that expertise in the coming year?
4. In your area of ministry, what concerns yet exist for the coming year?
5. List your major goals for this present year and comment on the progress that has been achieved. Supply specific data, if possible.
6. List the educational or professional opportunities you have participated in this year. Identify any such opportunity that would be beneficial for you in preparing for your ministry needs next year.
7. What are the strengths of the present staff? What are the weaknesses?

Personal Experience
1. What makes our church of particular interest to you?
2. What do you consider to be the most significant event that has occurred for this congregation this year? For you, personally?
3. Describe the manner and materials you used to maintain your personal spiritual walk with God this year.
4. In what ways could the church board/your supervisor be most supportive to you in preparing for another year of ministry at our church?
5. How have your ministry position and responsibilities impacted your family this year?

Select a rating on the scale provided for the following concepts:
1. Your agreement with the stated goals of our church.

    Minor　1　2　3　4　5　6　7　Significant

2. Your agreement with your present job description.

    Minor　1　2　3　4　5　6　7　Significant

3. Your ability to provide the necessary leadership and skills to your present activities in our church.

    Minor　1　2　3　4　5　6　7　Significant

4. Your comfort with staff procedures.

    Minor　1　2　3　4　5　6　7　Significant

5. Your success at recruiting, motivating, and retaining volunteers to fulfill the needs of ministry.

    Minor　1　2　3　4　5　6　7　Significant

6. Your ability to obtain necessary materials for effective ministry.

   Minor   1   2   3   4   5   6   7   Significant

7. Your comfort with the style and flow of the worship services.

   Minor   1   2   3   4   5   6   7   Significant

8. Your comfort with the style and flow of the administrative meetings of the church.

   Minor   1   2   3   4   5   6   7   Significant

9. Your satisfaction with the financial package our church supports.

   Minor   1   2   3   4   5   6   7   Significant

10. Your desire at this time to continue pursuing a staff position at our church for next year.

    Minor   1   2   3   4   5   6   7   Significant

—Adapted from a form used by Central Wesleyan Church,
Holland, Michigan.

NOTES

Chapter 1

1. Eugene Cernan and Don Davis, *The Last Man on the Moon* (New York: St. Martin's Press, 1999), 48.
2. Andrew Chaikin, *A Man on the Moon* (New York: Viking/Penguin Group, 1994), 1.
3. Ibid., 2.
4. Ibid.
5. Carl F. George, "Fulfilling God's Vision for Your Ministry," *Ministry Advantage*, July/Aug 1994, 8.
6. Elmer Towns, *The 8 Laws of Leadership* (Lynchburg, Va.: Church Growth Institute, 1992), 21.
7. Fred Smith, *Learning to Lead* (Waco, Tex.: Word Books, 1986), 34.
8. Rick Warren, *The Purpose Driven Church* (Grand Rapids, Mich.: Zondervan, 1995), 28.
9. Towns, *8 Laws*, 21.
10. J. Oswald Sanders, *Spiritual Leadership* (Chicago: Moody Press, 1967), 72.
11. Phil Stevenson, "An Unowned Vision Goes Unfulfilled," *Seedlings*, an inspirational e-mail message sent periodically by the author.
12. Cited by John Maxwell and Jim Dornan, *Becoming a Person of Influence* (Nashville: Thomas Nelson, 1997), 131.
13. Don Shula and Ken Blanchard, *Everyone's a Coach* (New York: Harper Business, 1995), 30.
14. "Helping Churches Articulate Vision: interview with Bill Hybels and Ken Blanchard," *Ministry Advantage*, Nov/Dec 1994, 4.
15. Warren, *Purpose Driven Church*, 118.
16. Shula and Blanchard, ibid.
17. Smith, *Learning to Lead*, 37.
18. Cited in *Maximum Leadership*, February 1996, 2.
19. Larry King, *How to Talk to Anyone, Anytime, Anywhere* (New York: Crown Publishers, 1994), 83.
20. Cited by Harvey Mackay, *Swim with the Sharks* (New York: William Morrow, 1988), 85.

Chapter 2

1. Richard L. Bergstrom, Gary Fenton, and Wayne A. Pohl, *Mastering Church Finances* (Portland, Ore.: Multnomah, 1992), 155.
2. "Successful Campaign Strategies," *Rev!*, Sept/Oct 2007, 52.
3. Robert Black and Ronald McClung, *1 & 2 Timothy, Titus, Philemon: A Commentary for Bible Students* (Indianapolis, Ind.: Wesleyan Publishing House, 2004), 108.
4. John Stott, *Guard the Truth: The Message of 1 Timothy & Titus* (Downers Grove, Ill.: InterVarsity Press, 1996), 137.
5. Dale Dauten, *Great Employees Only* (Hoboken, N.J.: John Wiley & Sons, 2006), 38.
6. Bergstrom, Fenton, and Pohl, *Mastering Church Finances*, 157.
7. Ibid., 158.
8. Jack Connell, "Anatomy of a Bad Hire," *Leadership*, Winter, 2006, http://www.ctlibrary.com/le/2006/winter/14.105.html (accessed December 2, 2008).
9. Herb Miller, "Financial Stewardship: Myths & Principles," *The Parish Paper*, June 2006.
10. "Giving to Churches Rose Substantially in 2003," *The Barna Update*, http://www.barna.org/FlexPage.aspx?Page=BarnaUpdate Narrow&BarnaUpdateID=161 (accessed October 23, 2008).
11. Miller, "Financial Stewardship."
12. Cited by Miller, "Financial Stewardship."
13. Cited by Robert H. Schuller, *Your Church Has Real Possibilities* (Glendale, Calif.: Regal, 1974), 29.

Chapter 3

1. Alastair Smith, *Election Timing* (Cambridge: Cambridge University Press, 2004), http://www.yale.edu/plsc506a/election timing.pdf (accessed November 11, 2008), 1–2.
2. Tony Campolo, *Let Me Tell You a Story* (Nashville: Word, 2000), 133.
3. Gordon MacDonald, "The Seven Deadly Siphons," *Leadership*, Winter 1998, 31.
4. John L. Mason, *An Enemy Called Average* (Tulsa, Okla.: Honor Books, 1993), 79.
5. Don Cousins, Leith Anderson, and Arthur DeKruyter, *Mastering Church Management*, (Portland, Ore.: Multnomah, 1990), 152.
6. Aubrey Malphurs, "Sharpening the Focus of Your Vision," *Ministry Advantage,* July/Aug 1994, 4.

7. Smith, *Election Timing*, 34.

8. Malphurs, "Six Key Qualities of a Vision Statement," *Ministry Advantage*, July/Aug 1994, 5.

Chapter 4

1. Pat MacMillan, *Hiring Excellence* (Colorado Springs: NavPress, 1992), 35–36.

2. Gary L. McIntosh, *Staff Your Church for Growth* (Grand Rapids, Mich.: Baker, 2000), 51.

3. Cited by MacMillan, *Hiring Excellence*, 38.

4. Ibid., 25.

5. Ibid., 46.

6. Gary L. McIntosh, *Biblical Church Growth* (Grand Rapids, Mich.: Baker, 2003), 99.

7. Bill Hybels, *Courageous Leadership* (Grand Rapids, Mich.: Zondervan, 2002), 81.

8. Cited by McIntosh, *Staff Your Church for Growth*, 55.

9. Hybels, *Courageous Leadership*, 84.

10. Ibid.

11. Alan Nelson, "Ministry in 2018," *Rev!* Jan/Feb 2008, 52.

12. McIntosh, *Staff Your Church for Growth*, 62.

13. *Men of Action*, Fall 1994.

14. Don Cousins, "Working Through Leaders," *Growing Your Church Through Training and Motivation*, Marshall Shelley, general editor (Minneapolis, Minn.: Bethany, 1997), 35.

15. Cited by John Maxwell, *Developing the Leaders Around You* (Nashville: Thomas Nelson, 1995), 54.

Chapter 5

1. Cited by Pat MacMillan, *Hiring Excellence* (Colorado Springs: NavPress, 1992), 132.

2. Ibid., 133.

3. Ibid., 169.

4. Ibid., 163.

5. Kenneth Chafin, *The Communicator's Commentary: 1, 2 Samuel* (Dallas: Word, 1989), 134.

6. MacMillan, *Hiring Excellence*, 160.

7. Ibid., 149.

8. Ibid., 193.

9. Ibid., 200.

10. David L. McKenna, "Reference Checking Workshop," Seattle, Wash., June 6, 2002.

Chapter 6

1. Norman Shawchuck, "A Candid Letter to Senior Pastors," *Leadership*, Summer 1980, 85.

2. Mary Jane Wilkie, "Medieval Methods," *Your Church*, July/August 2008, http://www.christianitytoday.com/yc/2008/ 004/3.29.html (accessed November 25, 2008).

3. Wayne Jacobsen, "Seven Reasons for Staff Conflict," *Leading Your Church Through Conflict and Reconciliation* (Minneapolis, Minn.: Bethany, 1997), 115.

4. David Lyons, "Staffing FAQs," *Rev!* Mar/Apr 2007, 66.

5. http://store.churchlawtodaystore.com/20cohaforchs.html (accessed November 26, 2008).

6. Wilkie, "Medieval Methods."

7. James Berkley, "How Pastors and Associates Get Along," *Leadership*, Winter 1986, 111.

8. Wilkie, "Medieval Methods."

9. Shawchuck, "A Candid Letter."

10. Jacobsen, "Seven Reasons," 122.

11. Cited by Shawchuck, "A Candid Letter," 87.

12. Berkley, "Pastors and Associates."

Chapter 7

1. Cited by John C. Maxwell, *The 21 Irrefutable Laws of Leadership* (Nashville: Thomas Nelson, 1998), 125.

2. Dale Dauten, *The Gifted Boss* (New York: William Morrow, 1999), 6.

3. Hans Finzel, *The Top Ten Mistakes Leaders Make* (Wheaton, Ill.: Victor Books, 1994), 25.

4. Cited by Finzel, *Top Ten Mistakes*, 41.

5. John Maxwell and Jim Dornan, *Becoming a Person of Influence* (Nashville: Thomas Nelson, 1997), 194.

6. *USA Today*, May 18, 1999.

7. John R. W. Stott, *Guard the Truth: The Message of 1 Timothy & Titus* (Downers Grove, Ill.: InterVarsity Press, 1996), 136ff.

8. Greg Asimakoupoulos, "Icons Every Pastor Needs," *Leadership*, Fall 1999, 109.

9. Cited by Stott, *Guard the Truth*, 138.

10. Robert Black and Ronald McClung, *1 & 2 Timothy, Titus, Philemon* (Indianapolis, Ind.: Wesleyan Publishing House, 2004), 109.

11. Stott, *Guard the Truth*, 141.

12. Don Cousins, Leith Anderson, and Arthur DeKruyter, *Mastering Church Management* (Portland, Ore.: Multnomah, 1990), 141.

13. Kenneth Blanchard, Patricia Zigarmi, and Drea Zigarmi, *Leadership and the One Minute Manger* (New York: William Morrow, 1985), 30.

14. Thomas E. Armiger, "Who Needs Coaching?" *The Wesleyan Advocate*, November 2002, 8.

15. Cited by Finzel, *Top Ten Mistakes*, 103.

16. *USA Today*, May 18, 1999.

17. Finzel, *Top Ten Mistakes*, 187.

18. Fred Smith, *Learning to Lead* (Dallas: Word, 1986), 33.

19. Gordon MacDonald, *Forging a Real World Faith* (Nashville: Thomas Nelson, 1989), 181.

20. Ibid.

Chapter 8

1. Fred Smith, "Understanding the Three Church Systems," *Renewing Your Church Through Vision and Planning* (Minneapolis, Minn.: Bethany, 1997), 105.

2. Stan Toler, *Stan Toler's Practical Guide for Pastoral Ministry* (Indianapolis, Ind.: Wesleyan Publishing House, 2007), 195.

3. Maxie Dunnam, *The Communicator's Commentary: Galatians, Ephesians, Philippians, Colossians, Philemon* (Waco, Tex.: Word, 1982), 206.

4. Gary L. McIntosh, *Staff Your Church for Growth* (Grand Rapids, Mich.: Baker, 2000), 20ff.

5. Cited by McIntosh, *Staff Your Church for Growth*, 31.

6. Smith, "Understanding the Three Church Systems," 113.

Chapter 9

1. Warren Lamb, "Hidden Treasure," http://sermoncentral.com/print_friendly_illustration.asp?illustration_id=62284 (accessed December 12, 2008).

2. "Andrew Carnegie—A Greater Than One Leadership Profile," http://studentlinc.typepad.com/studentlinc/2005/11/andrew_carnegie.html (accessed December 12, 2008).

3. Cited by Bobby McDaniel, http://sermoncentral.com (accessed December 13, 2008).

---

4. Todd Rhoades, "The Changing Face of Church Staffing," *Rev!* Mar/Apr 2007, 61.

5. Ibid.

6. Ibid., 62.

7. Pat MacMillan, *Hiring Excellence* (Colorado Springs: NavPress, 1992), 54.

8. Ken Heer, *Luke: A Commentary for Bible Students* (Indianapolis, Ind.: Wesleyan Publishing House, 2007), 99.

9. Rhoades, "The Changing Face," 63.

10. Jim Collins, *Good to Great* (New York: Harper Business, 2001), 42.

11. Wayne Jacobsen, "Kindling Their Vision," *Growing Your Church Through Training and Motivation* (Minneapolis, Minn.: Bethany, 1997), 210.

12. Collins, *Good to Great*.

13. C. Peter Wagner, *Leading Your Church to Growth* (Ventura, Calif.: Regal, 1984), 213–214.

14. Alan Miller, "Some Things are Worth Preserving," *The Triangle* (Marion, Ind.: Indiana Wesleyan University, 1999), 47.

15. Bill Hybels, *Courageous Leadership* (Grand Rapids, Mich.: Zondervan, 2002), 126–127.

16. Robert H. Schuller, *Move Ahead with Possibility Thinking* (Old Tappan, N.J.: Fleming H. Revell, 1973), 17–18.

17. Tony Campolo, *Let Me Tell You a Story* (Nashville: Word, 2000), 162.

18. Lee Strobel, *God's Outrageous Claims* (Grand Rapids, Mich.: Zondervan, 1997), 156.

Chapter 10

1. Cited by Gary L. McIntosh, *Staff Your Church for Growth* (Grand Rapids, Mich.: Baker, 2000), 9.

2. Mike Murdock, *The Leadership Secrets of Jesus* (Tulsa, Okla.: Honor Books, 1996), 96.

3. Bill Hybels, *Courageous Leadership* (Grand Rapids, Mich.: Zondervan, 2002), 124.

4. Stan Toler, *Stan Toler's Practical Guide for Pastoral Ministry* (Indianapolis, Ind.: Wesleyan Publishing House, 2007), 173.

5. Don Cousins, Leith Anderson, and Arthur DeKruyter, *Mastering Church Management* (Portland, Ore.: Multnomah, 1990), 113.

6. Murdock, *Leadership Secrets*, 91.

7. McIntosh, *Staff Your Church for Growth*, 97–99.